Leaning i.

"From the origin of Christianity, Halstead reminds us that disciples have consistently leaned into God's embrace through contemplative practices. Certainly, traditional practices of prayer remain beneficial in expressing our concerns and anxieties, hopes and dreams, blessings and regrets. This transformative book, however, leads us into stillness and silence, centering our hearts on the presence of God and ushering us into awareness of the work of the Spirit in our lives."

    —**David W. Wray,** associate dean of Spiritual Formation, cocurriculum emeritus, and codirector of ACU Summit, Abilene Christian University

"There are few people I know who've spent as much time contemplating the role of intentional prayer as Jackie Halstead. This book is the fruit of much thinking, doing, and being. For all who are thirsty to drink from purer water sources, this is an important book."

    —**Joshua Graves,** preaching and teaching minister, Otter Creek Church, author of *The Feast*

"In this volume, Jackie Halstead introduces key spiritual guides from past ages, lays out a pathway of basic spiritual formation practices, and unpacks a treasure trove of tools for further research. So if you have just stepped onto the 'spiritual formation pathway,' or if you are a seasoned pilgrim at midcourse, or if you are a spiritual guide for others, *Leaning into God's Embrace* is the book for you."

    —**Dr. Lynn Anderson,** pastor, teacher, and author

"Halstead's beautiful work provides a deep dive into growing closer to God, trusting God, and loving God. Techniques of embracing, learning, and teaching others how to let Scripture and prayer lead are shared; Halstead passionately discusses varied styles of contemporary and ancient contemplative prayer, guiding the reader to inner peace and quiet listening. If God has not opened the eyes of your heart to solitude for important conversations and prayer, these strategies are invaluable."

    —**Norma Bond Burgess,** associate provost of Diversity, Inclusion, and Special Initiatives, Lipscomb University

"In *Leaning into God's Embrace*, Dr. Jackie Halstead meticulously explains spiritual disciplines as tools designed to equip us to engage in what she describes as passive prayer wherein God sets the agenda. She maintains that in the posture of active listening to God, the longing in the heart finds satisfaction in its discovery that the heart's ultimate longing is to sense its belonging to God. In this historic period of pandemic, extreme anxiety, loss, and death, I find Jackie's invitation as a welcomed reminder of the refreshing hope we have in God who is our spiritual habitat."

—**Jerry Taylor,** founding director of the ACU Carl Spain Center on Race Studies & Spiritual Action

LEANING INTO
GOD'S EMBRACE

LEANING INTO
GOD'S
EMBRACE

A Guidebook for Contemplative Prayer

JACKIE L. HALSTEAD

LEAFWOOD
PUBLISHERS
an imprint of Abilene Christian University Press

LEANING INTO GOD'S EMBRACE
A Guidebook for Contemplative Prayer

L E A F W O O D
P U B L I S H E R S
an imprint of Abilene Christian University Press

Cataloging-in-Publication Data is on file at the Library of Congress, Washington DC.

Cover design by Bruce Gore
Interior text design by Strong Design, Sandy Armstrong

Leafwood Publishers is an imprint of Abilene Christian University Press
ACU Box 29138
Abilene, Texas 79699

1-877-816-4455
www.leafwoodpublishers.com

22 23 24 25 26 / 7 6 5 4 3 2

Contents

Foreword   by Randy Harris 9

Chapter One   A Foundation for Contemplative Prayer 13

SECTION ONE
Praying with Scripture

Chapter Two   Divine Reading (*Lectio Divina*) 29

Chapter Three   Imaging Prayer (Imaginative Contemplation)............... 39

Chapter Four   Praying the Divine Hours 49

SECTION TWO
Praying with the Body (Embodied Prayer)

Chapter Five   Body Prayer... 63

Chapter Six   Fasting.. 71

Chapter Seven   Walking the Labyrinth 83

Chapter Eight   Creation Prayer 91

Chapter Nine   Anglican Prayer Beads
(Protestant Prayer Beads or Anglican Rosary)............ 101

Chapter Ten   Journaling Prayer... 113

Chapter Eleven   Art as Prayer.. 121

SECTION THREE
Other Prayers of the Church

Chapter Twelve   Iconography.. 131

Chapter Thirteen   Process of Examen 137

Chapter Fourteen   Centering Prayer....................................... 145

Chapter Fifteen   The Jesus Prayer.. 151

Chapter Sixteen   Stations of the Cross 157

Chapter Seventeen   Practicing the Presence.............................. 179

Conclusion   Rule of Life... 183

Acknowledgments   191

Foreword

I suppose if you are a hammer, the whole world looks like a nail. Contemplative prayer has been such an important part of my own journey with God that I have been known to say it would cure virtually all the spiritual ills that infect us. I have discovered that is not true. Sometimes you need a really good, warm, chewy chocolate chip cookie too. But I digress . . .

When the history of late twentieth century theology is written, I am quite certain that my mother will not be on the list of the greats or near greats. But her theological instincts were keen, and I still remember a conversation that must have taken place nearly forty years ago. She said something like the following: "When people ask us how to become a Christian, we know exactly what to tell them to do. On the other hand, when they ask us how we draw closer to God, we don't know quite what to tell them, so we give them the big two: read your Bible and pray. And somehow it comes off a bit hollow."

Now no Christian can raise an objection to reading the Bible and praying. I have spent the last year reading the whole Old Testament from a new excellent translation. It has been a rewarding experience and a learning one, but it hasn't always brought me closer to God. I recently finished Zechariah and didn't understand a word of it. And somehow, much of our praying gets stuck in the realm of asking for God's blessing on our long list of agenda items. Is this what we mean by "read your Bible and pray"?

This brings me to this excellent book on contemplation. As the author points out, the idea itself of contemplative prayer needs a little explaining, and she does a fine job of doing this. I will merely point out that as I have talked to churches about contemplative prayer, there are two objections that are consistently raised. First, isn't this Buddhist stuff? I have studied Buddhism somewhat in the Academy and retreated at several Buddhist monasteries and retreat centers, including a retreat with perhaps the greatest living Zen master. I have learned much from those experiences and am grateful. They do have some basic techniques in common, but they come from totally different thought worlds. Dr. Halstead is not just calling us to be mindful but to pay attention to the loving God who makes himself known in Jesus Christ—the God whom Jesus calls by the intimate title father. The second objection that is often raised is, isn't this Catholic stuff? Well, in several instances, yes. Some of these practices, though by no means all, have been most at home in the Catholic Church. But many of them have been around for thousands of years and proven to deepen the spiritual lives of those who engage them. To reject them because they were nurtured in a different branch of the Christian church is shortsighted to say the least. I can't help but wonder what would happen if all the various sects and denominations were able to share the best of themselves with the rest of the Christian household and then have those other Christians embrace the best rather than the worst that we have to offer. What difference might that make in the world?

So I offer this book as a partial answer to my mother's question of how we grow closer to God. Dr. Halstead, far from rejecting the notion that we should read our Bible and pray, actually provides practical instruction in *how* we might do that. In doing so, as far as I can tell, there is not a single new idea in this book. And I assure you that's a good thing. I am not against new spiritual practices, per se, but everything that is suggested in this book has been tested by centuries of Christian practice. The whole Christian tradition bears witness to the practices in this book. Some of these approaches may be new to you, but they are all time-tested and proven from centuries of Christian exploration.

When you are exploring new practices, it is always wise to have a competent guide. For the author, these practices are not theory but a way of life. She has explored the territory she is inviting you into. You will be in good hands.

Finally, I hope you will notice how grounded this book is in the most basic Christian theological commitment: incarnation. Christianity is defined by our belief that God took on flesh and dwelt among us in Jesus Christ. This book lays out a spirituality that is embodied. To deny or denigrate our embodiedness is to reject the most fundamental truth of our faith. There is no room for a spirituality that is esoteric or ghostly. The practices in this book call upon us to follow our Savior who came *in the flesh*.

I cannot help being drawn back to this lovely verse from John Greenleaf Whittier's wonderful hymn, "Dear Lord and Father of Mankind":

O Sabbath rest by Galilee!
O calm of hills above,
Where Jesus knelt to share with Thee

The silence of eternity
Interpreted by love!

For this book turns out to be a love story. The relentless love of God transforms the human being into his loving partner. We discover whom we were created and intended to be and find the deepest and richest life possible in the love of God expressed in Jesus Christ. It turns out that when God looked at his creation and declared it to be good, he was exactly right.

Randy Harris

Author of *Living Jesus* and *Daring Faith*, and
Senior Consultant and University Fellow,
Siburt Institute for Church Ministry

CHAPTER ONE

A Foundation for Contemplative Prayer

A number of years ago, I was teaching a class on the theory and practice of prayer. It was a week-long intensive course, and we spent the first day talking about contemplative prayer. It was new to some of the seminarians, and one student, John, wrestled with incorporating this perspective into his framework for prayer. He left class in a state of dissonance and had trouble sleeping that evening. He and his wife had a number of horses and mules, and on that particular evening, he decided to go out and spend some time with them. He thought this might give him some time to think through some of the new concepts.

Among these animals were several "rescue mules." These animals, rescued from abusive situations, were brought to John for care and rehabilitation. One of the mules was named "Tiger" because of a pattern of stripes on his legs. Tiger had been severely abused before his rescue, and when he was given to John, the person who turned him over said, "This is one of the meanest animals I have ever encountered. I don't know if you can do anything for him." But John and his wife decided to give him a home and see if they could help. For the next two years, Tiger kept his distance. He was smart and quickly learned that he didn't need to fight with the other animals. However, he wanted nothing to do with humans. He stayed as far away as possible when anyone came into the corral to feed or care for him and his stablemates.

That evening after our class, John was in the corral grooming and talking with the horses and mules. He loved the animals, and it was a place of solace for him. As he threw a blanket over one horse, he felt a nuzzle at his ear. He assumed it was one sweet mare who tended to love on whoever came her way, but when he turned his head to look, to his surprise it was Tiger! For some reason, Tiger decided that night that he trusted John and wanted to be with him. For the two hours that John was in the corral that late night, Tiger never left his side.

The next morning, John relayed this story to the class. As he finished recounting, he exclaimed with excitement, "God spoke to me through Tiger! He gave me an example of contemplative prayer. It's not about talking; you just want to be with God. It's about the joy of being in God's presence!"

What a beautiful way to describe contemplative prayer! It *is* about relishing the presence of God. We don't have to say a word—in fact, it's better if we remain silent. We want to create a space where we won't miss anything that God may have to say to us!

Contemplative prayer allows us to follow the admonition of the psalmist to "Be still, and know that I am God" (Ps. 46:10). It is analogous to standing still after walking in a stream. When we stop moving, the silt settles and the water becomes clear. This form of prayer offers the opportunity to silence the distractions (both external and internal) and center our focus on God. When we are still, we are able to listen. This is what we are made to do! For centuries, the church has been utilizing various forms of contemplative prayer—a vast treasure of methods that have been honed through the ages. We find them in the writings of the desert mothers and fathers, in the collected works of monastic communities, and in the teachings of the church mothers and fathers. What a joy that in recent years, this form of prayer has made a resurgence—perhaps due to our deep need for the stillness that it offers. The modern norm is to live at a frantic pace, but now more than ever, we need the opportunity to focus our attention on and relish God's presence.

What Is Contemplative Prayer?

What exactly is *contemplative prayer?* Some have described it as *passive prayer*, in contrast with *active prayer. Active prayer* is prayer in which we set the agenda. We decide the content. This prayer includes components articulated by acronyms such as ACTS (adoration, confession, thanksgiving, and supplication) or PRAY (praise, requests, adoration, and yielding). *Contemplative prayer*, on the other hand, is the listening side of prayer. It is being with God in a manner that allows God to set the agenda. In his book *Living in the Presence*, Tilden Edwards states that contemplative prayer is about being still and letting God answer—sometimes with words but most often with a loving presence. He goes on to define contemplative prayer as "a state of quiet appreciation, simply hollowed out for God."[1]

This appreciation is cultivated as we recognize through this listening stance that God's presence is a gift. It is not something we make happen. Our role is to be receptive and accept the grace. We develop a special quality of awareness.

Before we begin to learn about its various forms, I want to lay an underpinning for contemplative prayer. We begin with a number of essential assumptions that incorporate a theological foundation for these practices.

An Active and Engaged God

The first assumption is that God is living and active in this world. One cannot participate in this form of prayer through the lens of deist philosophy—that God set the world in motion and then left us to fend for ourselves. Instead, we must recognize the reality that God is intimately involved with each of us and is always present. This may seem obvious, but it is unfortunately a common trend for believers to face life as if we are alone. Parker Palmer coined the phrase "functional atheism" for the manner in which the behavior of many Christians parallels that of those who are atheist.[2] We live as if the ultimate responsibility for all rests on us. We do not act as if we believe the God of the universe is present in each moment. Our actions and thoughts convey a hopelessness that should be reserved for those who do not know God. This is not a conscious decision but is how we live when the distractions of our busy lives keep our eyes off of God. The remedy is to remember—to develop a constant awareness of God's presence.

The importance of remembering that our God is alive is a long-standing issue that appears throughout the narrative of Scripture, in both the Old and New Testaments. For example, the prophet Habakkuk spoke to the people about why interaction with idols, the gods of the day, was so inherently different from contact with the true living God. He emphasizes the logical response of silence before the *living* God:

> "Of what value is an idol carved by a craftsman?
>> Or an image that teaches lies?
> For the one who makes it trusts in his own creation;
>> he makes idols that cannot speak.

Woe to him who says to wood, 'Come to life!'
    Or to lifeless stone, 'Wake up!'
Can it give guidance?
    It is covered with gold and silver;
    there is no breath in it."
The LORD is in his holy temple;
    let all the earth be silent before him. (Hab. 2:18–20)

Habakkuk tells us that when we come before God, our logical response is silence. We talk before a god that is not real, as that god, of course, cannot speak. But when we encounter the *living* God, we are quiet. God may have something to say to us.

The Psalms support this instruction. We have already touched on the teaching of the psalmist—"Be still, and know that I am God" (Ps. 46:10). Another example from Psalms is "Be still before the LORD and wait patiently for him" (Ps. 37:7). We still our mouths, minds, and bodies and are attentive to God because God is alive!

Albert Edward Day once observed that God seems unreal to most of us, even though he is actually "nearer to our hearts than our own feelings."[3] Day gave the example of an encounter with a friend who is lost in thought while walking toward us. This friend is not aware of us until we intentionally bump into them. Even though we are right in front of them, they are unconscious of our presence until we collide with them. Day makes the point that this is similar to the manner in which we are unaware of God until some event or tragedy almost forces us to recognize that God is present. Even though we believe that God is with us, we allow the many things vying for our attention to consume us. We forget about God.

It is when we remember that God is with us that we live in a different way. We cannot help but respond to the richness of life to which we are invited. Day states, "What makes life splendid is the constant awareness of God. What transforms the spirit into his likeness is intimate fellowship with him. We are saved—from our pettiness and earthiness and selfishness and sin—by conscious communion with his greatness and love and holiness."[4]

A Desire to Follow

A second assumption undergirding contemplative prayer is that as Christians we are committed to following the practices of Jesus. We look to Jesus for our model for *being*. Jesus held a regular practice of being in solitude with God—so much so that we recognize he was, most likely, not just talking *to* God but savoring the presence of his Father. The Gospels are filled with examples of this practice. In the Gospel of Mark, Jesus spends time with God at the start of the day. The previous day had been spent teaching, casting out demons, and healing. It was a very full day of ministry, and he was likely weary. But the Gospel writer tells us, "Very early in the morning, while it was still dark, Jesus got up, left the house and went off to a solitary place, where he prayed" (Mark 1:35). Another instance is in the Gospel of Luke. The Gospel writer tells us that before Jesus chose his disciples, he went out to a mountainside to pray and spent the night praying to God (Luke 6:12). And in another chapter, Luke relays that when increasing numbers of people were seeking Jesus to hear him and be healed by him, he "often withdrew to lonely places and prayed" (Luke 5:16).

It would appear that Jesus was able to maintain his center in the midst of his busy schedule due to this flow between ministry and time with God. Henri Nouwen portrays this pattern of life as Jesus moved from solitude to community to ministry in an article entitled "Moving from Solitude to Community to Ministry."[5] Nouwen wrote that this pattern is in contrast with the typical practice of many who approach a life of ministry. Often a ministry is launched with an idea followed by the inclusion of others who support that idea. The whole ministry is in place before the step of turning to God in prayer. Jesus, however, reversed that sequence. Nouwen uses an example of a day in the life of Jesus to illustrate the pattern (Luke 6:12–19). Jesus started with solitude as he spent the night in prayer. He needed close communion with his Father before one of the most important decisions of his ministry. He then moved into community as he chose those who would walk with him as disciples. Finally, they went out together and ministered.

Nouwen places great emphasis on the significance of this sequence—especially the first phase. Jesus first spent time alone with God. It is the manner in which we become grounded in God and come to recognize our identity as that of a beloved child of God. As we then move into community, we are not tossed to and fro by the approval of others. We can let their opinions go because we know who we are in God. This grounding of our identity in Christ happens as, over time, we come to know and be shaped by God as we spend time with him. It does not happen without intentional time set aside.

A final example of Jesus's pattern of being with God is found in the Gospel of Matthew. When Jesus learned from John's disciples that John had been beheaded by King Herod, Jesus "withdrew by boat privately to a solitary place" (14:13). This news was a terrible blow to Jesus. He lost a person who was very dear to him—his cousin, his forerunner, and the man who baptized him. John was perhaps the only living person who understood who Jesus was and what he was about. The family of Jesus didn't understand him. At one point, they were going to take him away because they thought he was crazy. His disciples didn't seem to fully understand until after the coming of the Holy Spirit on the day of Pentecost. When John died, it was a terrible loss for Jesus.

We read that when Jesus heard the news of John's death, his first inclination was to go to a solitary place. He needed time with his Father to grieve this sorrow. Unfortunately, we see as the narrative continues, he was not able to be in solitude. The crowds followed. When Jesus saw them, he had compassion and began healing and teaching. This was a lengthy process. When Jesus healed a person, he did so individually by speaking to them and touching them. He gave them his personal attention. Thus this day of healing continued into the evening. But it was not over yet! Jesus then told his disciples to feed the crowds, and we see the feeding of the five thousand. This was another time-intensive occurrence. It most likely took a good deal of time to distribute the bread and fish, for the crowd to eat, and for the remains to be gathered—not a speedy occurrence.

So, we see that Jesus had a significant emotional blow at the beginning of the day as he was informed of the death of John, tried to get away, but was then waylaid by a full day of ministry. But, finally, finally, at the end of this long day, he had a chance to be alone with God. The passage tells us, "Immediately Jesus made the disciples get into the boat and go on ahead of him to the other side, while he dismissed the crowd. After he had dismissed them, he went up on a mountainside by himself to pray. Later that night, he was there alone" (Matt. 14:22–23). Again, Jesus went to a solitary place to be with his father. He needed time with God to find comfort.

These examples illustrate that the practice of going to a solitary place to pray was part of the regular routine of Jesus. Again, this was not prayer in the sense of Jesus talking the entire time. I can certainly imagine Jesus pouring out his heart, but for the bulk of the time, I see him leaning into his Father's embrace and allowing God to love and sustain him. He looked for opportunities for this. It was his sustenance.

This pattern of Jesus resonates with me personally. I have been blessed by a number of silent retreats—experiences that were affirmed when I saw the rhythm lived by my Lord. I began going on these weekend silent retreats in order to hear various speakers. I certainly benefited from the presentations, but the true blessing of these retreats was the discovery of the practice of solitude and silence. Apart from the presentations, the participants were expected to honor the silence. It was wonderful! The depth of communion with God was something I had longed for but had yet to experience. In the silence, I felt the layers stripped away. I was no longer able to distract myself from the voice of God, and God gently taught me how to listen.

Gradually, a rhythm developed. When I settled in at the retreat center, I would begin to release the things that I was carrying—worries, anxieties, my list—and I would finally "arrive." As I let go of these distractions, my struggles, sins, and pain rose to the surface, where God and I could address them together. This experience was never harsh, although I met it with trepidation. If I sensed a challenge from God, it was a gentle chiding followed by a release as I would again recognize God's unending love for me. Through this and beyond, I would lean into God's embrace and drink in the love.

I wept profusely for the first few retreats. My tears flowed unchecked for the entire weekend. It was not unpleasant, just unusual for me. I wasn't sure what to make of it. I later learned that this was the gift of tears—a cleansing. In addition, I realized that being in silence and solitude was more than sitting still with my hands folded. In contrast, I spent most of my time outside walking, sitting, journaling, and sketching. My experience of prayer expanded. And, most importantly, I learned how to listen in prayer.

A Positive Perspective

A final assumption undergirding contemplative prayer is related to our perspective of God or at least our desire to have a positive relationship with him. It does not make sense that I would entrust myself to a God whom I perceive as angry or uncaring. If this was the case, I might make a half-hearted attempt to spend time with him because I "should." But this attempt is difficult to sustain when deep down I do not want to be with God. I may first need to address and heal this image before I can rest easily in the arms of God.

Benedict of Nursia, one of the church fathers in the late fifth century, wrote a *rule of life* for those in monastic communities. It was a guide on living in community in a godly manner and addresses everything from the practicalities of eating and sleeping to the more spiritual topics of prayer and Scripture. At the heart of this rule is a chapter on humility that addresses one's developing relationship with God. Benedict believed humility and spiritual development to be two sides of the same coin. He used the image of a ladder in describing this journey to spiritual maturity. He stated that on the bottom rungs of the ladder (the beginning of our spiritual journey), the focus of our attention is on ourselves. I want to know what I will get out of a relationship with God. It is egocentric—as it should be! Why would I want to enter into a relationship if I am not getting something out of it? Yet as I continue to climb the ladder, my attention begins to expand beyond myself. As I come to appreciate God, I want to share this relationship with others. This loving God has blessed me, and I want to invite those I love to know God. I am focused on others and how they can join me on this journey.

However, the ladder does not stop there. As I continue to climb, my gaze becomes increasingly fixed on God. My desire becomes one of wanting to be fully available for God's use. God is at the center, and my life revolves around God's work in this world. Paradoxically, I become freer as I ascend the ladder yet also grow in humility. My desire is progressively tied to the things of God. As we have all experienced, this climb is not lineal but a spiral. There are times when I reach a place of dissonance and my focus shifts back to myself. But I gradually move up the ladder as I mature in my relationship with God.

Unfortunately, what often moves us up the ladder are times of suffering. In my life, I have faced this refining in numerous ways. One such occurrence happened a number of years ago when my husband was a minister for a church. We had a two-year-old daughter, and I was pregnant with our second daughter. We lost this baby in stillbirth, and I was devastated. I didn't know how to make sense of the loss. Up until this point in my life, I had not been faced with significant hardship. I had always been faithful to God to the best of my ability and couldn't understand why God would repay my loyalty with allowing my baby to die. I didn't believe that God caused the death but knew God certainly could have prevented it.

I decided that God didn't deserve me and turned away from him. No one knew this, not even my husband. I was good at the "game" of being a Christian. I continued to teach both children and adult classes. I represented the church in the community and continued living the active life of a minister's wife. Yet I was keenly aware of my distance from God. I had never existed apart from God, and I was terribly lonely. I hung on to my hurt and anger for three long years. When I finally came to my senses, it was because of this loneliness. I realized that the only thing worse than going through the pain of losing a child was going through it without God. I was still angry and didn't understand why God allowed it to happen, but I realized that my relationship with God was more important than understanding the ways of God. It was a turning point in my life as I returned to God and decided I wanted to be part of God's work in this world. I would be God's servant, rather than expecting God to be my servant. This shift happened as a result of this deep pain.

This trajectory is certainly not unique to me. Many have discovered the deeper meaning of being in relationship with God through suffering. It changes our perspective and our focus. It is often in difficult times that we come to know God more fully. My image of God changed, albeit unconsciously, to recognize that God is in control. And I continue to relearn this periodically as I take the reins of control again and again, allowing myself to slip back into the center of my world.

Ready to Receive

This book is a love story—primarily about learning to open ourselves to God's love. Each prayer that is included herein encourages a letting go and a posture of attention. In a sense, we are with God in a stance of listening. It's the comfortable silence with which we commune with those we love. Words are not needed—being in the presence of each other is enough. In this form of prayer, we let God set the agenda. It is our role to show up.

It may seem passive—it is, in fact, referred to by some as "passive prayer"—but in reality, it requires effort. We are opening ourselves to the shaping work of the God of the universe, and as we do so, God peels away the layers of distraction.

My first exposure to contemplative prayer felt like coming home. A deep longing for God was occasionally met for me through study, prayer, and communion with the church. My repertoire for being with God, however, was limited. I did not have language for the listening side of prayer, nor a means to create space to be with God in this manner. Fortunately, I found the language and the way as God led me to teachers—both ancient and contemporary—who taught me about contemplative prayer. I cannot express the level of gratitude I have for this grace, and it is my hope that you will find this same gift from God.

This book offers instruction in answering the deep longing we have for a relationship of deep intimacy with our God. We were made to be in relationship with the Creator. The psalmist described it as follows: "You, God, are my God, earnestly I seek you; I thirst for you, my whole being longs for you, in a dry and parched land where there is no water" (Ps. 63:1). This longing can only be filled by a deep union with God. Nothing else will suffice. The prayer forms discussed in this book allow us to lean into God's loving embrace. You may be surprised at some of the prayers that are included. Each fulfills the condition of helping us let go of control and listen. Our job is to lean into God's embrace. God does the rest. Contemplative prayer increases our awareness of God's presence. When I live with this constant awareness, I live in a way that manifests God's love. This prayer is part of the paradox of growing deeper in our relationship with God. There is nothing that we can do to deepen this relationship; it is all a gift from God. However, we can make ourselves available for God's shaping. This is the function of contemplative prayer. The various forms that are discussed in the following chapters offer tools to assist us in being still so we can remove distractions and let God shape us.

Practice

In preparation for entering into the prayers of this book, create a space in your home that will serve as your routine quiet place. It should be comfortable, well lighted, and removed from distractions. Have a journal, your Bible, a pen, simple art supplies, and other materials that will allow you to settle in quickly each time.

Begin with a few minutes of silence and offer your time to God. Let go of your worries, concerns, and lists in this moment, and settle into your time with God.

Notes

[1] Tilden Edwards, *Living in the Presence: Spiritual Exercises to Open Our Lives to the Awareness of God* (New York: HarperOne, 1995), 11.

[2] For more about "functional atheism," see Parker J. Palmer, *Let Your Life Speak: Listening for the Voice of Vocation* (San Francisco: Wiley & Sons, 2000).

[3] Albert Edward Day, *Discipline and Discovery* (Nashville: Upper Room, 1947).

[4] Day, *Discipline and Discovery*.

[5] Henri J. M. Nouwen, "Moving from Solitude to Community to Ministry," *Leadership Journal* 16, no. 2 (1995): 81–87.

PRAYING WITH SCRIPTURE

Eugene Peterson speaks of two ways of reading in *Eat This Book*. When one is reading for *information*, one is taking in content with the aim of learning, such as reading a newspaper. We read "lightly" as we skim, and then maybe stop and read more closely. We gain knowledge. This is an important approach as we engage with Scripture. It is vital that we know the Word—God's written revelation. That is how we come to comprehend the story of God and God's kingdom. We learn of the servants and ways of God and seek to emulate these servants. It is also the way in which we create a foundation to ground ourselves in the character of God. When faced with other revelation, we place it alongside the understanding we have gained through our reading of Scripture to determine if the revelation fits what we know of God.

God's written revelation is living and active, and we are changed as we ingest it. We have times of insight as the Word speaks to us at a deep level. Students of Scripture cannot help but be altered even reading for information. Yet there are ways to be in Scripture that are *intentionally* transformative. This is the other method of reading noted by Peterson. It is easier to grasp when one thinks of a love letter. This type of writing is read in a much different way than that of a newspaper. One pours over the letter and reads it slowly and carefully—almost caressing it with the mind. It is read repeatedly, and the words are cherished. Another analogy used by Peterson is that of a dog worrying (or "gnawing") a bone. The dog delights in this treat and chews on it for a time. He then buries it in a secret place and comes back to it repeatedly to chew on it some more. This is reading for *transformation*. We read in ways that take us deep into the essence of the Word. We allow the Word to *read us*. Peterson quotes the poet Rainer Maria Rilke as he describes this form of reading: "[The reader] does not always remain bent over his pages; he often leans back and closes his eyes over a line he has been reading again, and its meaning spreads through his blood."[1]

These ways of engaging with Scripture can be described as forms of contemplative prayer. We let go of our agenda and give control to God. We let the *Word read us.* We open ourselves to whatever it is that God may have for us through God's revelation in Scripture.

Note

[1] Eugene H. Peterson, *Eat This Book: A Conversation in the Art of Spiritual Reading* (Grand Rapids: Wm. B. Eerdmans, 2009), 1–4.

CHAPTER TWO

Divine Reading

(*Lectio Divina*)

The words *Lectio Divina* **literally mean "divine reading."** It is a form of contemplative prayer in which we read Scripture in a slow, meditative manner. This is one of the forms to which Eugene Peterson referred as reading in a *transformative* manner.[1]

I have learned a number of "tricks of the trade" in my thirty-plus years as a marriage and family therapist. The first stage of therapy involves establishing rapport with the client. I want to make them comfortable and aware that they are in a safe place—a place in which they can be honest and vulnerable. This process requires that I "read" the client. If they are anxious, I adjust my delivery to help them calm down. I slow down my speech, talk in a calm manner, and give them plenty of time to ease into the session. If they are angry and accusatory, I assess the reason behind this. Are they afraid? Have they been forced to come? Through questioning and aligning myself with the client, I let them know I am on their side and that they have nothing to fear. This ability to read the client allows me to assist them to the best of my abilities.

Eugene Peterson tells us that *Lectio Divina* is one way in which we allow Scripture to "read" us. As we read in a meditative, unhurried way, we descend from the head to the heart. We enter into a time of focusing our attention on God. The Creator knows us more intimately than we know ourselves. As the Spirit leads us through this method of being in Scripture, we relinquish control and release ourselves into the care of our God.

Background and History

Reading Scripture in a meditative way has been practiced throughout the history of the church. As previously mentioned, Benedict of Nursia wrote a rule of life for monastic living. It was essentially instruction on how to live in community in a godly manner. One of the three primary disciplines required of the monks was the meditative reading of Scripture. They approached this task with reverence. Writings, including the sacred text, were rare, and this may have contributed to the practice. The few available copies were shared. The typical requirement was three hours of meditative reading of Scripture each day.

Guigo II, a Carthusian monk in the twelfth century, systematized meditative Scripture reading into its contemporary form.[2] He laid out four stages that entail repeated reading of the text— *lectio*, *meditatio*, *oratio*, and *contemplatio*. The Latin titles for these stages continue to be utilized.

Lectio, or reading, is the first stage of the practice. It is the reading of the passage. Thelma Hall states that this is not textbook reading but meditative reading. She states of the stage of *lectio*, "[It is] reading with a listening attitude, and with a willingness to personalize the words so that they are read as though God is speaking directly to the reader."[3] She suggests that all historical practices of this form required readers to maintain an erect posture to ensure their attentiveness to the *living* Word of God. Thus we prepare ourselves to be attuned to the Speaker and to listen with fresh ears and an open heart.

The second stage, *meditatio*, is a time of meditation or thinking. In this stage, the imagination is used to draw from and expand upon what has been read. This is when the reading becomes personal. We enter into the reading and hear it offered specifically to us. I sense the love that God has for me and I listen. I listen for a word or phrase to rise up—to be given to me. This, again, is recognizing that I do not control the prayer; God does. I let go and allow the mystery of this relationship to touch me.

Oratio, speaking/responding, is the stage described as the prayer of the heart. As we continue to let go of our need to control, we move from our intellect into our heart. We realize the longing we have for God and open ourselves to this loving relationship. It is a vulnerable stance—naked before our Creator. As we become aware of this desire for God, our desire deepens and our longing increases. The distractions fall away, and God becomes our center. We open ourselves to God to speak to the happenings in our current life. We listen for an invitation.

Finally, *contemplatio*, or contemplation, is a time of being with God. The previous stages are defined by our activity. We are now still, resting quietly in God's embrace. We move from *doing* to *being*. We let go of everything we know and cling to—fear and doubt, joy and happiness—and allow our true selves to emerge. It is a time of inward darkness, as we do not understand where God is leading us. Yet from this darkness comes a piercing sense of God's presence—an awareness that, as John Tyson suggests, deepens our longing for God's presence.[4] In this stage, we are releasing our hold on ourselves to give God space to shape us into his likeness. In this, we experience true freedom.

French Benedictine monk Dom Marmion captures the heart of the stages in the following poetry:

We read	*(Lectio)*
Under the eye of God	*(Meditatio)*
Until the heart is touched	*(Oratio)*
And leaps to flame.	*(Contemplatio)*[5]

In my journey with contemplative prayer, *Lectio Divina* was one of the first forms of the practice that I encountered. I felt a level of comfort with this way of being with God, as it involved my beloved Scripture. I was familiar with the Bible from the time I was a child and had experienced transformation from God through its pages. This process of divine reading was the easiest to step into.

I don't, however, remember the first time I experienced *Lectio Divina*. It may be that my natural inclination to pair the reading of Scripture and interaction with God allowed the process to feel organic. What I do know is that the practice helped me move from a guilt-induced "annual reading of the Bible" to this slow, meditative "worrying of the bone." I'm grateful for the many times I read through the Bible. It gave me a firm foundation on which to stand. Unfortunately, this annual reading had been reduced to a task on my checklist—a duty to gain entry into heaven. I had lost the pleasure of being in the Word.

Lectio Divina offered a fresh way to relish the text and became part of my regular practice. I have used it with many passages throughout the entire Bible—both Old and New Testaments. I have also selected a few favorite texts that I come back to again and again. It never ceases to amaze me how the Spirit knows what I need to receive and nuances the insights given—understandings that differ based on my situation and context.

Lectio Divina, along with all contemplative prayer forms, can be prayed alone or in community. It is important to create a context that facilitates a calm, safe space. It should be free from distractions, comfortable, and with adequate light for reading. A candle can be lit as a symbol of the presence of the Holy Spirit.

The text will be read four times. It is important to use the same translation each time to allow for the movement from head to heart.

Praying Alone

- Allow between twenty minutes and an hour for this prayer. (Setting an alarm helps keep track of the time.)
- Find a quiet place, free from interruptions.
- Get in a comfortable position and take everything off your lap.
- Place both feet on the floor, in order to give yourself a sense of grounding.
- Offer the time to God and ask for God's guidance.
- Close your eyes and take a deep breath, breathing in God's love and light. Breathe out any worry or anxiety, along with concern about your work, home, or relationships. Breathe in God's love, letting it fill every crevice. Take a couple of breaths like this.
- Follow this format:

Lectio (read)

- As you enter into the first reading, listen with fresh ears and an open heart. Listen as if you've never heard it before.
- Read the passage of Scripture in a slow, meditative manner.

- On your second reading, listen attentively for a word or phrase that seems to be given to you—a word that draws you to it.
- Read the passage a second time.
- Sit in silence for one or two minutes.

Meditatio (meditate)

- On your third reading, allow the Spirit to bring to your mind and heart an experience or issue that you are facing right now—one that seems to connect to your word or phrase. Do not force it; just allow it to emerge.
- Read the passage a third time.
- Sit in silence for one or two minutes.

Oratio (speak/respond)

- On the final reading, listen for an invitation. Is God inviting you to do or be something in the coming days?
- Read the passage a fourth time.

Contemplatio (contemplation)

- Spend a few minutes (five to twenty) resting in God's presence.
- As you gain comfort in the method of prayer, increase your time in silence at the end.

Leading a Group

When leading a group, it's helpful to walk them through the entire process before beginning. They then know what to expect and are able to settle into the prayer. Consider saying something along these lines: "I'm going to read the text four times. I'll give you the instructions throughout, so you don't have to remember them. The first time I read the text, try to hear it with fresh ears and an open heart—as if you've never heard it before. The second time, listen for a word or phrase to arise—as if it is given to you. The third time, listen for a context in your life that seems to relate to the word or phrase. And the fourth time, listen for an invitation. Is God inviting you to do or be something in the coming days? Then we'll enter into a time of silence when you imagine yourself leaning into God's embrace. I'll let you know when it's time to stop."

Then, say the following in a slow, meditative manner: "Get in a comfortable position with both feet on the floor. Have nothing in your hands or lap. Hold your hands in an open posture on your knees. Close your eyes and take a deep breath, breathing in God's love and light. Let it flow through you. Breathe out any anxiety or worry you are carrying about your home, job, family, or relationships. Again, breathe in God's love and light. See it fill every crevice of your body. Breathe out any darkness or sadness. Take a couple of breaths like this."

You can pause as the group breathes in this manner and then continue with the instructions. Remember to maintain an unhurried, calm pace when giving the instructions and reading the text.

Lectio (read)

- Instructions for the first reading: "Remember to listen with fresh ears and an open heart. Listen as if you've never heard it before."
- Read the passage of Scripture in a slow, meditative manner (first reading).
- Instructions for the second reading: "Now as I read it a second time, listen attentively for a word or phrase that seems to be given to you—a word that draws you to it."
- Read the passage again (second reading).
- Sit in silence (one or two minutes).

Meditatio (meditate)

- Instructions for the third reading: "Now, as I read this a third time, allow the Spirit to bring to your mind and heart an experience or issue that you are facing right now—one that seems to connect to your word or phrase. Do not force it; just allow it to emerge."
- Read the passage again (third reading).
- Sit in silence (one or two minutes).

Oratio (speak/respond)

- Instructions for the fourth reading: "As you listen this final time, is God inviting you to do or be something in the coming days? Listen for an invitation. We'll then spend a few minutes resting in God's presence. I'll let you know when to stop."
- Read the passage again (fourth reading).

Contemplatio (contemplation)

- Sit in silence (five minutes).

Invite members to share the word/phrase or invitation they heard from God. Emphasize that they share only what they feel comfortable sharing. If the group is large, divide them into groups of three or four to share before returning to the large group.

Concluding Thoughts

One of the rich blessings that comes with *Lectio Divina* is the opportunity to experience Scripture in new ways. As mentioned previously, it allows us to descend from our head to our heart, giving us an openness to the unique intent of the Spirit for our lives and context.

Additional Resources

Casey, Michael. *Sacred Reading: The Ancient Art of Lectio Divina.* Liguori, MO: Triumph, 1995.

Hall, Thelma. *Too Deep for Words: Rediscovering Lectio Divina.* New York: Paulist Press, 1988.

Peterson, Eugene H. *Eat This Book: A Conversation in the Art of Spiritual Reading.* Grand Rapids: Wm. B. Eerdmans, 2009.

Notes

[1] Eugene H. Peterson, *Eat This Book: A Conversation in the Art of Spiritual Reading* (Grand Rapids: Wm. B. Eerdmans, 2009), 3.

[2] For more details on the origins of liturgy and Scripture reading, see Philip Sheldrake, *Spirituality: A Brief History*, 2nd ed. (Chichester, West Sussex: Wiley-Blackwell, 2013), 42.

[3] Thelma Hall, *Too Deep for Words: Rediscovering Lectio Divina* (New York: Paulist Press, 1988), 36.

[4] John R. Tyson, ed., *Invitation to Christian Spirituality: An Ecumenical Anthology* (Oxford: Oxford University Press, 1999), 49–50.

[5] Hall, *Too Deep for Words*, 44.

CHAPTER THREE

Imaging Prayer
(Imaginative Contemplation)

Imaging prayer is another form of contemplative prayer that makes use of God's revelation in Scripture. In this prayer form, we use our imaginations to enter into an event in Scripture—most often an event in the life of Jesus. Like *Lectio Divina*, it is an additional way in which we allow "the Word to read us."

Having a firm footing in Scripture is vital to imaging prayer. This textual grounding allows for a firm grasp of the character of God—vital awareness to lay alongside the experience of prayer. We thus seek to know God through both an intimate knowledge of the details of Scripture as well as the Word in its entirety. N. T. Wright speaks of Scripture as a narrative in five acts.[1] These acts together offer an encompassing picture of the faithfulness and love of God. Act One is the story of creation. The creation portrays the desire of the Trinity to bring this world (and universe) into being. It was made with beauty and creativity. We were created in love. This was made clear when humanity was given free will to love God or reject God.

Act Two tells of the fall of humanity. We fell from God's perfect purpose for us. We were created to walk intimately with God, but we chose to turn away. What God asks of us is to recognize our dependence on him and allow him to be our security. God is with us! We are the children of God. In this Act, we see that God does not abandon us in our fallenness. God continues to love humanity.[2] Act Three continues this theme as we are given an understanding of God's relationship with Israel. God's plan to reconcile all people through his son, Jesus, was brought to fruition through God's people—the Israelites. We see through this relationship that God pursued his people. They were unfaithful time after time, yet God's faithfulness is manifest in his continuing relationship with them.

Act Four tells of the new covenant through Jesus. God came in the flesh and lived among us. This was the ultimate step of reconciliation. Jesus showed us how to live—how to treat people, what to value, and how to live in this hurting world and triumph. We live this out in Act Five as the body of Christ. We, the church, are commissioned to continue the work he began. God partners with us to make us useful instruments of the kingdom. Our role is to be available to God. God does the shaping. We make manifest the purposes of Christ—righteousness, peace, joy, love, and mercy. In this last Act, we recognize that we are included in the story of God. Our life and relationship with God contribute to this narrative of love.

This thirty-thousand-foot view is important to maintain, while at the same time diving into the details in Scripture. The details allow for an intimate understanding of the particulars. As we develop familiarity with the text, it becomes embedded in our hearts, and the Spirit can recall it when needed or helpful. It is a "both/and" philosophy in which we relish both the forest and the trees.

This perspective is vital, as we use our imaginations to enter into the events in Scripture, for two reasons. First, we can lay any insight we receive alongside the character of God, which we have come to know through our study of Scripture. If we have an insight that is not consistent with God's character, we recognize that the insight is not *of* God. Second, our image of God influences how we are with God. As I come to know God as love through this overarching story of Scripture, I develop a trusting relationship with God. I am then open to receive what God may have for me.

Without this understanding of God, I am susceptible to the dissonance caused by difficult texts and stories in Scripture. I will want to distance myself from God and will find it difficult to be vulnerable in prayer. Why would I want to be with a God who I do not like or trust? But the more all-encompassing understanding of God as love affords me the opportunity to weather these hard texts and emerge with an intimate relationship with God.

Thus I come to imaging prayer (or any prayer, for that matter), ready to open myself to whatever it is that God may have for me. I trust in the faithfulness and goodness of God and know that even if the message is difficult, I will be blessed. I can enter into the process of imaging prayer, also referred to as "imaginative con-templation," with openness and eagerness to have this experience with Jesus.

Background and History

Imaging prayer came to us from Ignatius of Loyola, the founder of the Jesuits or Society of Jesus. He was a wealthy young man who lived in sixteenth-century Spain. He had the advantages of wealth and a place in the royal court as an apprentice to the king's treasurer. He was said to be vain, good with the ladies, and valiant in battle. His future was secure as a prominent member of the elite.

A shift in this future occurred when Ignatius was wounded in battle. He was struck in the leg by a cannonball and spent a year convalescing in the family castle.[3] His recovery was long, and he had his leg rebroken when it began to heal in a crooked way. (He did not want to be unattractive in his tights.) He had little to distract himself during this lengthy convalescence, except for the two books that were available in the castle. One was on the life of Christ, and the other was an accounting of the lives of the saints.

Always a competitive one, Ignatius began to compare himself to the saints. He imagined performing acts of valor for the Lord and for the church. These fantasies were paired with thoughts of his life in court, victory on the battlefield, and winning the heart of a noble lady. He recognized in these fantasies the significant impact of his imagination—both in enticing him into the life of the court and in drawing him to a relationship with Christ. This was the precursor of the *Spiritual Exercises*, a thirty-day journey in being with Christ and a vital component of the training of the Jesuits. Through these exercises, a spiritual director leads a directee through four stages of a journey. Imaginative contemplation comes into play as the directee prays with Scripture and allows herself to enter into the events of the life of Christ through imagination. Directees experience their lives and thoughts alongside the life, suffering, and ultimate victory of Jesus.

After experiencing weekend retreats for a number of years, I was encouraged by a Jesuit priest to take a longer retreat. It is the practice of the Jesuits to embark on an annual eight-day retreat, and this is what my friend urged me to do. Three-day retreats were beneficial, but a longer amount of time would allow for a deeper, richer time of listening.

I thus began taking an eight-day silent retreat each year. These are directed by a Jesuit priest and include the practice of imaging prayer. Each day during the retreat, I meet with the director for an hour of spiritual direction. We talk about my life and relationship with God, and the director assigns a number of texts with which to pray. These often include a psalm and a text from the Gospels that connect with my life experience. As I pray with these scriptures, I enter into the events with my imagination.

For example, when feeling alone in a difficult situation, I spend time with the Good Shepherd as he searches for the lost lamb. I may envision myself as the lamb who thrills to hear the Shepherd calling my name. I feel him lift me onto his shoulders and experience the safety of his embrace. Or when wrestling with a decision, I sit with Mary at the feet of Jesus. I recognize that there is nothing more important in that moment than giving my full attention to whatever he has to say to me. When in grief, I walk along with the disciples as they listen to Jesus on the road to Emmaus. I experience his companionship as we walk along and listen with wonder to his explanation of Scripture. We break bread together, and I am thrilled when I recognize that he is my Lord! Of course, there is not a designated text for each issue I face. But there are some that dovetail nicely with my concerns. As with *Lectio Divina*, the Word reads me and the Spirit ministers to me in different ways at different times. This form of prayer has had a profound impact on my life and relationship with Christ.

PRACTICE

As the name implies, when we pray with imaging prayer, we imagine ourselves in the event in Scripture. We enter fully in by utilizing our senses—sight, hearing, touch, and smell. This assists us in the encounter with Christ. It brings a freshness to the text as we experience it in a new way. We encounter Christ in a way that is much closer than when we simply read *about* Jesus. Any narrative in the life of Jesus can be used with this prayer form.

Praying Alone

- Allow between twenty minutes and an hour for this prayer. (Setting an alarm helps keep track of the time.)
- Find a quiet place, free from interruptions.
- Get in a comfortable position, and take everything off your lap.
- Place both feet on the floor in order to give yourself a sense of grounding.
- Offer the time to God and ask for God's guidance.
- Close your eyes and take a deep breath, breathing in God's love and light. Breathe out any worry or anxiety, along with concern about your work, home, or relationships. Breathe in God's love, letting it fill every crevice. Take a couple of breaths like this.
- Read the text two times in a slow, meditative manner. Try to read it as if you have never read it before—with fresh eyes and an open heart. Let your curiosity and wonder come alive.
- Now, set aside the Bible and close your eyes. Enter into the event with all your senses—your sight, your hearing, your touch, and your smell. Imagine yourself in the scene.
- End by taking time alone with Jesus. You can just sit with him and drink in his presence, or you can have a conversation with him. Do not try to control your thoughts; just let them go where they will.

The following is an example using the story of Jesus healing the woman with the hemorrhaging disease in Mark 5:24–34.

- Read the event two times in a slow, meditative manner.
- Set your Bible aside, but stay in the event.
- What do you feel?
  - Is the weather hot? Do you feel a breeze?
  - Can you feel the ground under your feet?
  - Do you feel the fabric of the clothes of those around you, brushing against you?
- What do you smell?
  - Animal smells?
  - Body odor?
  - Is it a dusty day?
- What do you hear?
  - The cacophony of the voices of the crowd?
  - Animal sounds? Birds?
  - The voices of the disciples arguing with Jesus?
  - The voice of Jesus?
- What do you see?
  - Is the sky blue?
  - Do you see the crowd? The disciples?
  - Do you see the woman touching the hem of Jesus's garment?
  - The face of Jesus?
- And where are you in the event?
  - Are you in the crowd?
  - Are you standing with Jesus?
  - Are you the person in need of healing?
- Stay right there and let everything fade but you and Jesus.
  - Go to him.
  - Sit beside him.
  - Talk with him or just be with him. Don't try to control it.
  - Spend the rest of the time with him.

Spend some moments journaling about your experience, or talk with another and share what happened.

Leading a Group

Give the following instructions (say all in a slow, meditative way):

- "Get in a comfortable position, and take everything off your lap."
- "Place both feet on the floor in order to give yourself a sense of grounding."
- "If you want, you can open your hands on your lap as a gesture of openness."

It's helpful to walk your group through the entire process before beginning. Then they will know what to expect and will be better able to settle into the prayer.

- "I'm going to read the text two times."
  - "The first time I read it, listen with fresh ears and an open heart—as if you have never heard it before."
  - "After I read it a second time, you should enter into the event using all your senses—sight, hearing, touch, and smell. I'll walk you through the experience."
  - "Then you will spend some time with Jesus."
- "Close your eyes and take a deep breath, breathing in God's love and light. Breathe out any worry or anxiety, along with any concern about your work, home, or relationships. Breathe in God's love, letting it fill every crevice. Take a couple of breaths like this."

Read the text in a slow and meditative manner.

Then, read it a second time.

Give the following instructions (continue using a slow, meditative voice):

- "Keep your eyes closed."
- "Now enter into the event."
- "What do you feel?"
  - "Is the weather hot? Do you feel a breeze?"
  - "Can you feel the ground under your feet? The fabric of the clothes of those around you?"
- "What do you smell?"
  - "Animal smells? Body odor?"
  - "Is it a dusty day?"
- "What do you hear?"
  - "The cacophony of the voices of the crowd?"
  - "Animal sounds? Birds?"
  - "The voice of the disciples arguing with Jesus?"
  - "The voice of Jesus?"
- "What do you see?"
  - "Is the sky blue?"
  - "Do you see the crowd? The disciples?"
  - "The woman touching the hem of Jesus's garment?"
  - "Jesus?"
- "And where are you in the event?"
  - "Are you in the crowd?"
  - "Are you standing with Jesus?"
  - "Are you the person in need of healing?"
- "Stay right there and let everything fade but you and Jesus."
  - "Go to him."
  - "Sit beside him."
  - "You can talk or just be with him. Don't try to control it."

- "Spend the rest of the time with him."

When the time has ended, sound a chime or say, "Okay, the time has ended."

- Ask participants to share with the person next to them. (The experience is enhanced through sharing with others, but sharing with one person is less intimidating than sharing with the entire group.)
- Ask for a couple of volunteers to share with the entire group. (This allows the group to share the experience together.)

Concluding Thoughts

St. Teresa of Avila was once asked, "How do I know insight is from God and not just my imagination?" She replied, "How else can God speak to us if not through our imagination?"

Additional Resources

Ignatius of Loyola. *The Spiritual Exercises of St. Ignatius: Or Manresa.* New York: TAN Books, 1999.

O'Brien, Kevin. *The Ignatian Adventure: Experiencing the Spiritual Exercises of St. Ignatius in Daily Life.* Chicago: Loyola Press, 2011.

Notes

[1] N. T. Wright, *The Last Word: Beyond the Bible Wars to a New Understanding of the Authority of Scripture* (New York: HarperCollins, 2005).

[2] See Elisabeth Sifton, ed., *Reinhold Niebuhr: Major Works on Religion and Politic* (New York: Library of America, 2015), 263.

[3] Philip Sheldrake, *Spirituality: A Brief History*, 2nd ed. (Chichester, West Sussex: Wiley-Blackwell, 2013), 127.

CHAPTER FOUR

Praying the Divine Hours

Praying the divine hours is a liturgy, or set script, for praying through the hours of a day. It is comprised of psalms, other readings from Scripture, and prayer, offering a means to bathe the entire day in prayer.

"Beneath the busyness of our lives, Someone waits for us to come home to who we truly are. All it takes is a simple pause to get us in touch with the One who keeps vigil with us."[1] With these words, Macrina Wiederkehr introduces the spirit of praying the hours in *Seven Sacred Pauses: Living Mindfully through the Hours of the Day.* The practice offers a sacred rhythm throughout the day that repeatedly reminds us of who we are and whose we are. Praying the divine hours is an act of entering global prayer. Although the hours vary based on time zones, we are participating in the same prayers around the world. And we are joining hearts with Christians throughout the centuries as we enter into Psalms—the prayer book of Jesus.

My religious upbringing taught me to be suspicious of liturgy. The belief was that if we read the prayers of others, our prayer is not genuine. Although the intent is sound in encouraging prayer from the heart, there is a rich treasure of prayer that is missed here. Great meaning can be derived from the rote prayer found in liturgy. The words become my words—speaking the deep emotion of my heart. It takes me deeper into God's embrace as those who have gone before me invite me into the baring of their souls to God.

Background and History

There are many names for this form of prayer: praying the hours, the divine hours, the liturgy of the hours, canonical prayer, and the daily offices. Regardless of the preferred title, praying the hours refers to the designation of various hours as hours of prayer. This practice was performed by the Jewish people as they prayed three times a day—morning, noon, and night. One example is the prayers of Daniel (Dan. 6:10–28).[2] The practice was so important to him that he was willing to risk his life in its fulfillment.

The practice was solidified for the church through the teachings of Benedict of Nursia in his rule of life. The monks were instructed to gather eight times—seven times during the day and once in the middle of the night. This pattern was based on the psalmist's teaching, "Seven times a day I praise you" (Ps. 119:164) and "At midnight I rise to give you thanks" (Ps. 119:62).[3] This form of praying the hours became the standard practice of monastic communities. As mentioned previously, spread throughout the day, this practice bathes the day in prayer and helps us remember that the day, and our work therein, belongs to the Lord. The prayers follow the arch of the day, and each has a theme coinciding with its placement in the day. These themes refer also to the arch of life, with the morning representing new life and the evening prayer suggesting death or the end.

Macrina Wiederkehr captures the Spirit of each hour in her book, *Seven Sacred Pauses*. They are as follows:

Vigils or *Matins* occurs in the middle of the night. It has the theme of "eternal longings" as we embrace the darkness in our lives.

Lauds is at the start of the day. It is a time to welcome the day. We prepare to bring God into our workday.

Terce is mid-morning and has the theme of "blessings." We pause in the middle of our morning to be thankful.

Sext is at high noon. It is the hour of courage, recommitment, and passion. We pray for peace for ourselves and for the world.

None is mid-afternoon and is the wisdom hour. It has faithfulness as its theme. We recognize God's faithfulness throughout the day.

Vespers is in the evening and is about balance. Our day of work has ended, and we invite play and prayer into our day.

Compline is right before we go to bed and has the theme of completion. We review our day and recognize God's hand in it.

Most Benedictine monastic communities now limit their gathered prayer to three of the offices: lauds, noonday prayers, and vespers. The rhythm of these three prayers aligns more suitably to our current world. If you have the opportunity to stay in a Benedictine retreat center, you will be blessed by the opportunity to participate with the brothers or sisters in this liturgy.

I have prayed the divine hours many times—both in community and alone. When staying in Benedictine monasteries or retreat centers, the sisters or brothers typically welcome me and other guests to pray alongside them in the chancel choir. They meet with me before I join them for the first time during a stay and walk me through the process. Then, when I join them for the hours, those sitting beside me help me when I get lost in the process. It doesn't take long before I fall into the rhythm of the process and join the beauty of the chanting.

When praying on my own, I use a couple of my favorite published versions of the hours. One is *Seven Sacred Pauses* by Macrina Wiederkehr (as cited previously). I was blessed to be at a retreat she was leading while she was in the process of writing this work. This little book captures the spirit of the hours. It is short and simple and has a lovely, poetic flavor. I also appreciate and often use the works of Phyllis Tickle, *The Divine Hours: Prayers for Springtime*, *The Divine Hours: Prayers for Summertime*, and *The Divine Hours: Prayers for Autumn and Wintertime*. Tickle's volumes are similar to the hours prayed in the monastic communities. These works and those recommended at the end of this section offer a rich framework for the day.

PRACTICE

Those who choose the practice of praying the hours on a daily basis are deeply impacted by this immersion in Psalms. It creates a rhythm that, like the monastic orders throughout the centuries, continually bathes their life and work in the kingdom. For the very ambitious, you can create your own offices. However, it is easiest to find a contemporary compilation of the hours in book form. Another source is a website (such as ExploreFaith.org) that offers an updated daily liturgy based on your time zone.

Praying Alone

As you begin, take time to center by beginning with silence and offering the time to God. Each office (hour) is a liturgy that includes prayers, psalms, and other textual readings. They are best read aloud or chanted. Augustine of Hippo (354–430) is credited with the phrase, "He who sings [i.e., chants] prays twice." When we chant, we pray with both our thoughts and our bodies as we give voice to the words of the Psalms. Chanting adds a rich beauty to the prayer form. A simple method is to choose a note or tone that is comfortable and say the entire line of verse in that tone. When you reach the end of the verse, you will note an asterisk. The asterisk serves two purposes—to designate a break in the verse and to instruct the pray-er to raise the tone one note on the last syllable before the asterisk. In the remainder of the verse, the original tone is followed with the last syllable of the verse being one note lower.[4]

Leading a Group

When leading a group in the divine hours, the same compilations can be used. Each participant will need a copy of the office to follow. There are a number of ways to lead the divine hours. One method is to assign the prayers and readings to different participants. They can speak or chant them, depending on their level of comfort. The entire group will say or chant the "refrain" together, along with the Gloria and the Lord's Prayer. In the following example, the group segments are in bold type. Note that only the Psalms are chanted (as noted by the asterisk at the end of the verse).

The office is approached with reverence—the group will enter in silence and leave in silence. For those new to the divine hours, include written instructions at the beginning of the liturgy or take some time to instruct the group at the beginning of the gathering. The following is an example I created of a morning office. (If using with a group, change the pronouns in the Prayer Appointed for the Week and the Benediction to the plural form.)

The Morning Office

Invitation to Prayer

Ascribe to the LORD, you heavenly beings,* ascribe to the LORD
   glory and strength.
Ascribe to the LORD the glory due his name;* worship the LORD
   in the splendor of his holiness. (Ps. 29:1–2)

A Request for Presence

You, God, are my God,* earnestly I seek you;
   I thirst for you, my whole being longs for you,* in a dry and
   parched land where there is no water. (Ps. 63:1)

The Greeting

I will exalt you, LORD,* for you lifted me out of the depths and
   did not let my enemies gloat over me.
LORD my God, I called to you for help,* and you healed me.
   You, LORD, brought me up from the realm of the dead;* you
   spared me from going down to the pit. (Ps. 30:1–3)

The Refrain

In God, whose word I praise—in God I trust and am not afraid.*
What can mere mortals do to me? (Ps. 56:4)

The Gospel Reading

Now Jesus learned that the Pharisees had heard that he was gain-
ing and baptizing more disciples than John—although in fact it
was not Jesus who baptized, but his disciples. So he left Judea and
went back once more to Galilee.

   Now he had to go through Samaria. So he came to a town in
Samaria called Sychar, near the plot of ground Jacob had given to

his son Joseph. Jacob's well was there, and Jesus, tired as he was from the journey, sat down by the well. It was about noon.

When a Samaritan woman came to draw water, Jesus said to her, "Will you give me a drink?" (His disciples had gone into the town to buy food.)

The Samaritan woman said to him, "You are a Jew and I am a Samaritan woman. How can you ask me for a drink?" (For Jews do not associate with Samaritans.)

Jesus answered her, "If you knew the gift of God and who it is that asks you for a drink, you would have asked him and he would have given you living water."

"Sir," the woman said, "you have nothing to draw with and the well is deep. Where can you get this living water? Are you greater than our father Jacob, who gave us the well and drank from it himself, as did also his sons and his livestock?"

Jesus answered, "Everyone who drinks this water will be thirsty again, but whoever drinks the water I give them will never thirst. Indeed, the water I give them will become in them a spring of water welling up to eternal life" (John 4:1–14).

The Refrain

In God, whose word I praise—in God I trust and am not afraid.* What can mere mortals do to me? (Ps. 56:4)

The Morning Psalm

Arise, LORD, and come to your resting place,* you and the ark of
   your might.
May your priests be clothed with your righteousness;* may your
   faithful people sing for joy.
For the sake of your servant David,* do not reject your
   anointed one.
The LORD swore an oath to David;* a sure oath he will
   not revoke:

"One of your own descendants* I will place on your throne.
If your sons keep my covenant and the statutes I teach them,*
   then their sons will sit on your throne for ever and ever."
   (Ps. 132:8–12)

The Refrain
**In God, whose word I praise—in God I trust and am not
afraid.* What can mere mortals do to me?** (Ps. 56:4)

The Lord's Prayer
**Our Father which art in heaven, Hallowed be thy name.
Thy kingdom come, Thy will be done in earth, as it is in heaven.
Give us this day our daily bread.
And forgive us our debts, as we forgive our debtors.
And lead us not into temptation, but deliver us from evil: For
   thine is the kingdom, and the power, and the glory, for ever.
   Amen.** (Matt. 6:9–13 KJV)

The Prayer Appointed for the Week
Lord of life and love, give me strength to live in the beauty of your
holiness. Quiet my soul and lift my eyes above the daily struggle of
life. Set my sight on you that I may know your grace manifest in
your Son, who lives and reigns with you and the Holy Spirit. **Amen.**

Benediction
God, you have brought me in safety to this new day. Empower me
to enter fully into your work and remain centered on your purposes and your Son. In his name we pray. Amen.

Concluding Thoughts
As you pray the hours, you will notice a cadence develops as you
let go of control and allow the practice to carry you into the beauty

of the liturgy. The framing of the day with these prayers brings you back again and again to your center. As with other forms of contemplative prayer, they will help you move from your head to your heart as you let go of the agenda and sink into God's loving embrace.

Additional Resources

Claiborne, Shane. *Common Prayer: A Liturgy for Ordinary Radicals.* New York: Zondervan, 2010.

Tickle, Phyllis. *The Divine Hours: Prayers for Autumn and Winter: A Manual for Prayer.* New York: Doubleday & Co., 2001.

———. *The Divine Hours: Prayers for Spring: A Manual for Prayer.* New York: Doubleday & Co., 2001.

———. *The Divine Hours: Prayers for Summer: A Manual for Prayer.* New York: Doubleday & Co., 2001.

Wiederkehr, Macrina. *Seven Sacred Pauses: Living Mindfully through the Hours of the Day.* Notre Dame, IN: Sorin Books, 2010.

Notes

[1] Macrina Wiederkehr, *Seven Sacred Pauses: Living Mindfully through the Hours of the Day* (Notre Dame, IN: Sorin Books, 2010).

[2] Gordon Mursell, ed., *The Story of Christian Spirituality: Two Thousand Years, from East to West* (Minneapolis: Fortress Press, 2001), 17.

[3] Justo L. Gonzalez, *The Story of Christianity*, vol. 2 (New York: HarperCollins, 2010), 280.

[4] For a more in-depth explanation of chanting, see the introduction of *The Divine Hours* by Phyllis Tickle.

PRAYING WITH THE BODY
(Embodied Prayer)

Early in the history of Christian spirituality, the concept of dualism was embraced. This belief suggests that there is a separation between the material and the spiritual. The spiritual was considered to be of God, and the material was evil. This principle came from the ancient Greek culture and was not accepted by the Hebrews or by early Christians.

Scripture, unfortunately, was used to substantiate this understanding. One text use, for instance, is Paul's injunction to avoid living according to the flesh, but to walk according to the Spirit. This sanction, however, was not meant to encourage this bifurcation but to encourage believers to live their lives motivated by the Holy Spirit rather than by self-serving attitudes. John Tyson states,

"Christian Spirituality does not signal a flight from physical life. . . . [R]ather it describes the processes whereby Christians seek to live holy lives, while in the flesh and while engaging the challenges of this world."[1]

This holistic philosophy was held by the ancient Hebrews in their view of the goodness of all of creation. Their Bible, the Old Testament, repeatedly attests to the virtuousness of creation. God himself pronounced that each aspect of the created physical world was "good" and that humans were "very good." The Psalms repeatedly attest to this goodness, in the recognition that creation cries out in praise of the character of God. "The heavens declare the glory of God; the skies proclaim the work of his hands" (Ps. 19:1).

In his book *Praying with the Body: Bringing the Psalms to Life*, Roy DeLeon speaks of the intimate bond between the physical and spiritual worlds that are seen in the Psalms. "You, God, are my God, earnestly I seek you; I thirst for you, my whole being longs for you, in a dry and parched land where there is no water" (Ps. 63:1). He goes on to speak of the teaching of Benedict to hold the body and soul as equal partners during prayer.[2] Paul speaks of this in his teaching to the Corinthians. "Do you not know that your bodies are temples of the Holy Spirit, who is in you . . . ? [Y]ou were bought at a price. Therefore honor God with your bodies" (1 Cor. 6:19, 20). Our body is to be an active participant in our spiritual journey. DeLeon writes that praying with our bodies

> allows us to fully acknowledge, appreciate, and praise
> God and his work [our body]. It also gives us the oppor-
> tunity to practice good stewardship of God's creation.
> For example, tight shoulders and neck muscles might
> inform us that we are not managing our stress levels
> well. . . . A shortness of breath might be a clue that we

are holding on to something, which calls for practicing patience or forgiveness.[3]

Christians are unique among the world faith traditions in the practice of leaving our bodies at the door of our places of worship. We engage with our minds and hearts but have lost the embodiment of our spirituality. This section of contemplative prayer has as its focus the inclusion of the body in prayer. Employing our bodies in prayer elicits a deeper meaning. We are present to God in a different way—impacted by the particular use of our bodies. As with other contemplative prayer forms, it allows us the opportunity to increase our awareness of God's presence.

Notes

[1]John R. Tyson, ed., *Invitation to Christian Spirituality: An Ecumenical Anthology* (Oxford: Oxford University Press, 1999), 4.

[2]Roy DeLeon, *Praying with the Body: Bringing the Psalms to Life* (Brewster, MA: Paraclete Press, 2009), vii.

[3]DeLeon, *Praying with the Body*, viii.

CHAPTER FIVE

Body Prayer

Body prayer, by definition, is incorporating our body into our prayer. It includes a spectrum all the way from laying prostrate before the Lord to the movement of the hands as they "walk" around the circle of Anglican prayer beads. Regardless of the method, prayer is enhanced through this inclusion.

What did Jesus do with his body when he prayed? As we look at Scripture, we see a variety of postures—none of which are the familiar mode of sitting with head bowed and hands clasped. Of course, there is nothing wrong with bowing our heads in a posture of humility. We are, after all, approaching the God of the universe. There are examples of *sitting* while praying, but these are also rare. The few instances we do see in Scripture portray an individual sitting before the Lord or the prophet of the Lord to receive instruction. An example is from the life of David, "Then King David went in and sat before the LORD and he said: 'Who am

I, Sovereign LORD, and what is my family, that you have brought me this far?'" (2 Sam. 7:18).

The majority of my body prayer experiences occurred when we were children—specifically in Vacation Bible School. We sang songs that integrated movement. I loved these experiences but left them behind as I became an adolescent. I was too cool for these childish activities. It was as an adult that I rediscovered more holistic perspectives of prayer, learning that at times my heart would follow my body in prayer. As stated by Jane Vennard in her book *Praying with Body and Soul*, my body becomes my teacher.[1] When I kneel, I first feel and then recognize the awe in coming before my Creator. When I lift my hands in prayer, I sense an opening, a giving of myself to God. These postures help me experience God in different ways through nonverbal messages. In addition, they keep my mind from wandering as I participate with my whole self. I am more receptive to what God brings me in prayer.

PRACTICE

Trying these various postures is a lovely way to experience the impact of each position. Experiment with each at different times and then come back to them when they match the heart you bring to prayer or the heart you *want* to bring to prayer.

Praying Alone

We begin our focus on body prayer with examples found in Scripture. There are a number of postures that are frequently cited.

Standing. Standing was a common practice of the Jews when they prayed. There were times when the entire assembly *stood* before the Lord. When King Jehoshaphat was afraid of the approaching armies of the Moabites, he *stood* and prayed. "All the men of Judah, with their wives and children and little ones, *stood* there before the

LORD" (2 Chron. 20:13—emphasis mine). When Hannah brought Samuel to dedicate him to service in the temple, she said, "Pardon me, my lord. As surely as I live, I am the woman who *stood* here beside you, praying to the LORD" (1 Sam. 1:26—emphasis mine). In the time of Jesus, he assumed the disciples would stand in prayer as he said, "And when you *stand* praying, if you hold anything against anyone, forgive them" (Mark 11:25—emphasis mine).

Standing in prayer communicates respect to God in a manner similar to that of standing with respect before a king or when an important person enters a room. This posture is appropriate for any time of prayer. It's the act of gazing into the eyes of God as you address or listen to God.

Lifting up hands. Another practice (that is often coupled with the act of standing in prayer) is the lifting up of hands. The psalmist writes, "May my prayer be counted as incense before You; The *lifting up of my hands* as the evening offering" (Ps. 141:2 NASB—emphasis mine). The writings of Paul also indicate, "Therefore, I want the men everywhere to pray, *lifting up holy hands* without anger or disputing" (1 Tim. 2:8—emphasis mine). This technique communicates humility and vulnerability as I come to God with open hands, ready to receive.

The lifting of hands can communicate a number of messages. One calls to mind the phrase of Isaiah, "Here am I. Send me!" (Isa. 6:8), as a logical intent. Another is a focus of praise and adoration as I reach my hands to the God I adore. Another is an openness to whatever it is that God has for me, such as in the offering of oneself at the beginning of a time of retreat.

I often utilize this prayer posture (standing with my arms lifted) in creation when I experience the magnitude of God's greatness. For instance, I frequent a retreat center in the Smoky Mountains. The buildings of this center are on a bluff overlooking a tree-filled valley surrounded by hills. My mind is captured in those moments, and I throw open my arms in response to a sense of awe for our Creator.

Kneeling. Another common stance of praying in Scripture is the act of kneeling. One example is given by the psalmist: "Oh come, let us worship and *bow down*; let us *kneel* before the LORD, our Maker!" (Ps. 95:6 ESV—emphasis mine). Paul also suggests the practice: "For this reason also, God highly exalted Him, and bestowed on Him the name which is above every name, so that at the name of Jesus every *knee will bow*, of those who are in heaven and on earth and under the earth, and that every tongue will confess that Jesus Christ is Lord, to the glory of God the Father" (Phil. 2:9–11 NASB—emphasis mine). Kneeling communicates surrender—humility.

This posture is a position of reverence. It is frequent in worship, as portrayed by the Psalms. It also elicits humility as we seek forgiveness or as, when feeling beaten down, we come to the Lord to be lifted up. Some churches incorporate kneeling into their service. They have kneeling benches that can easily be pulled down and put away several times during the liturgy. I find this practice to be meaningful. It deepens my experience of worship as we are invited to kneel for a prayer or during the Eucharist (the Lord's Supper).

In addition, I utilize a prayer bench in my home. It is stationed in front of a window with a place on which I can rest my arms. I go to this bench when I am particularly distressed and seeking help. The act of kneeling helps communicate my heartache.

Lying down. The Scripture provides a number of examples of lying down and praying while in bed. Here are two instances from the Psalms: "Tremble and do not sin. Meditate in your heart *upon your bed* and be still" (Ps. 4:4 NASB—emphasis mine). "When I remember You *on my bed*, I meditate on You in the night watches" (Ps. 63:6 NASB—emphasis mine). Praying in this manner (and in this place) is an offering of the darkness to God.

The examples we have of this posture, as shown in the Psalms, most often occur in the middle of the night. This is a time when concerns rise to the surface. I awaken in the darkness, and my fear overwhelms me. Praying while lying in bed is a way of claiming God's presence in our anxiety. God is at work while the world sleeps.

Prostrate. The final posture of prayer found in Scripture is a prostrate position. One particularly strong example comes from the contest between Elijah and the prophets of Baal, when fire miraculously rained down from heaven and consumed the altar and sacrifice: "When all the people saw it, they *fell on their faces*; and they said, 'The LORD, He is God; the LORD, He is God'" (1 Kings 18:39 NASB—emphasis mine). Another example is in the garden before Jesus was arrested. "And He went a little beyond them, and *fell on His face* and prayed, saying, 'My Father, if it is possible, let this cup pass from Me; yet not as I will, but as You will'" (Matt. 26:39 NASB—emphasis mine).

This position communicates humility and reverence. It is an expression of deep need and concern. I recognize my lowly state and seek to show my vulnerability before the God of the universe. An obvious use of this posture is coming to God when in deep emotional or physical pain. I cry out in distress and portray my absolute dependence on God.

Praying the Psalms with our bodies. Another way to use our bodies in prayer is to include postures as we say or sing the Psalms. These postures can come in the form of sign language or movements that hold personal meaning. As with the other suggested postures, the addition of our body allows us to experience the prayers of Jesus (the Psalms) with deeper significance.

One method is to create the postures and act them out. A number of artists have set the Psalms to music, thus allowing for an easy process of prayer. Fernando Ortego is one artist who has a number of albums that include psalms set to music. When movement is added to the music, they become dances of praise or lament.

DeLeon offers instruction in coupling body postures with the Psalms in *Praying with the Body: Bringing the Psalms to Life*. The following is one example of this with Psalm 63 (his book also includes drawings of body postures):

> My soul thirsts for you, my God,
> *Inhale: Breathing in slowly, drink in God's refreshing, revitalizing breath.*
> My body craves your living water.
> *Exhale: Let your body go limp as you exhale completely.*
> I lift up my heart to you,
> *Inhale: Open up your chest and offer your heart to God.*[2]

Leading a Group

When leading a group in praying with the body, there are a number of approaches to use. One way is to choose a posture for the group and process the experience together. For instance, if the chosen posture is kneeling, you might have the group kneel in prayer and then share the impact of that practice. Another method is to divide the group into small groups and let them choose a posture they will try together. Postures can also be assigned for practice during the week with the intent to report back on the experience. I used this latter approach when teaching prayer postures to undergraduate students in a course entitled "Disciplines for Christian Living."

They were assigned a posture to practice several times during the week. They journaled about the experience and shared their experiences with the class. The students were always surprised by the increased intensity of their emotions as they approached God with the various postures. One student was particularly impacted by the act of laying prostrate before God. He shared that he felt vulnerable and humble—a new experience for him.

Another method is to lead the group in a song with simple body movements. I choose a psalm and incorporate one movement per phrase (in a manner that is similar to the previously mentioned example from DeLeon). I practice a number of times in advance, in order to have a level of comfort and to work out the kinks in timing. For example, with Psalm 34:2–5 NASB:

> My soul will make its boast in the LORD;
>> (head thrown back and fist on chest)
>
> The humble will hear it and rejoice.
>> (hand to ear and bright smile)
>
> O magnify the LORD with me,
>> (arms stretched up to the heavens and swaying)
>
> And let us exalt His name together.
>> (hands cupped to mouth to project)
>
> I sought the LORD, and He answered me,
>> (straight hand over eyes as if searching)
>
> And delivered me from all my fears.
>> (arms hugging self and rocking back and forth)
>
> They looked to Him and were radiant,
>> (hands outstretched from face like the sun)
>
> And their faces will never be ashamed.
>> (hands over face and then dropping)

When leading the prayer, I demonstrate the movements and then have the group practice one time without the music. The music is then added, and we go through the song twice. The first time is to practice as they gain comfort in the movement. The second time allows for the actual experience of prayer. If possible, I bring the prayer back later in the retreat or on a following week when teaching a class. This, of course, can be done without music as well, but I find that pairing it with music allows for a more meaningful experience.

Concluding Thoughts

It is enriching to experiment with each of these postures. There may be some that resonate more fully than others as your personal posture of prayer. Or you may find that different seasons call for different postures. Having a variety at your disposal can allow for a new, rich interaction with God.

Additional Resources

DeLeon, Roy. *Praying with the Body: Bringing the Psalms to Life.* Brewster, MA: Paraclete Press, 2009.

Ortega, Fernando. "Oh God, You Are My God (Psalm 63)." *The Shadow of Your Wings: Hymns and Sacred Songs*, Curb Records, 2006.

Pagitt, Doug, and Kathryn Prill. *Body Prayer: The Posture of Intimacy with God.* Colorado Springs: Waterbrook Press, 2005.

Vennard, Jane E. *Praying with Body and Soul: A Way to Intimacy with God.* Minneapolis: Augsburg Press, 1998.

Notes

[1] Jane E. Vennard, *Praying with Body and Soul: A Way to Intimacy with God* (Minneapolis: Augsburg Press, 1998), eBook, line 155.

[2] Roy DeLeon, *Praying with the Body: Bringing the Psalms to Life* (Brewster, MA: Paraclete Press, 2009), 55.

CHAPTER SIX

Fasting

Fasting is another practice that helps us center on God. It is contemplative prayer in the sense that it assists us in listening to God. It does so in a number of ways. First, without the distraction of food—preparing, eating, cleaning up—we have increased space to attend to God. Second, we are participating in a discipline that gives us the opportunity to feast on the things of God. And third, we are bringing our body into submission and learning how to say "no" to our cravings—a practice that helps us say "no" to other urges.

Background and History

There are many definitions for fasting—abstinence from food, water, pleasures, social media, and so forth. The biblical definition of fasting is to abstain from food and sometimes from water. There is nothing wrong with other forms; they can result in significant blessing as we release our hold on things that consume our attention. However, for the purposes of this book, we will devote our attention to abstinence from food.

Scripture is rife with examples of fasting. It was part of the Jewish culture as we see in the Bible. King David fasted and prayed as he pleaded for the life of his son (2 Sam. 12:15–24). After his son died, he stopped and explained that he had been fasting in order to seek God's mercy for the life of his son. Esther had the country fast with her for three days as she prepared to risk her life in going before the king (Esther 4:16), and Jesus fasted for forty days as he prepared to be tempted (Matt. 4:1–2). Early Christians continued this Jewish tradition. They did not see their faith as a denial of their Jewish tradition but as a conviction that Christ was the long-awaited Messiah. Thus they continued many of the faith practices of their Jewish forefathers—including fasting. It was an act in which they expressed sorrow for their sin. One author, Justo Gonzalez, states that the typical fast days for the Jews were Monday and Thursday, but the early Christians moved the days to Wednesday and Friday—possibly to commemorate the betrayal and crucifixion of Jesus.[1]

Through the first few centuries, the church continued to practice fasting as penance and as preparation for baptism and Easter. The Second Letter of Clement, the earliest surviving sermon transcript written in the first century, states that "prayer, fasting, and almsgivings are the central activities that constitute Christianity and which turn the hearts of believers back to God." The Didache, a writing from around 130 AD, ordered disciples to fast for two or three days before baptism.[2]

Other church leaders through the centuries encouraged the practice of fasting as an expression of piety and act of denial. Jerome of Bethlehem (348–420) wrote letters of spiritual counsel that popularized Christian disciplines such as fasting. Martin

Luther (1483–1546) encouraged the use of fasting "that a man may rule his own body," and fasting was part of the conversion experience of Ignatius (1491–1556) as he underwent a weeklong fast in order to rid himself of the scruples and excessive guilt over his sins. Charles Wesley (1707–88) believed fasting to be one of the "ordinances of God to be obeyed by all who desired to commune with the saints." And Thomas Merton (1915–68) fasted in preparation for his baptism.

In all these examples, we see that fasting offered an opportunity for an intense time of interaction with God—a time of devotion, discipline, and listening. Unfortunately, the practice fell into disfavor in the Western Protestant Church. Richard Foster's *Celebration of Discipline* attributes this disfavor to a number of reasons. First, many Christians had a strong reaction against the abuse of the discipline in the Middle Ages through asceticism—a lifestyle of severe abstinence. Fasting became associated with this excess. A second reason is that the increasing affluence of the Western world discouraged any type of self-denial. It was much less demanding to choose a discipline such as giving rather than abstaining from food, even though in the New Testament, fasting is mentioned much more than giving. Finally, fasting declined in popularity for a time due to the belief that it was necessary to eat three meals a day for a healthy lifestyle.[3] This is no longer a popularized concept, but it still gives some pause as people consider the discipline.

The practice of fasting for *spiritual* purposes has made a comeback in recent years. The intent is similar to that found in Scripture—an act of self-denial and a sign of penance. It is often aligned with prayer as a matter of significance to the individual or faith community. Although not a specific command by Jesus, it was assumed that this was part of the worship of those he was teaching, typically accompanied by prayer and giving. For example,

Jesus said, "*When* you fast, do not look somber as the hypocrites do" (Matt. 6:16—emphasis mine).

Based on these examples in Scripture and through the ages of the church, we see a number of reasons to fast. The main purpose of fasting is to help center our lives on God. Everything is stripped away, leaving us space to focus on God. In his book *The Spirit of the Disciplines*, Dallas Willard states, "Fasting confirms our utter dependence on God as we find our sustenance beyond food. With fasting, we are feasting on God." He goes on to say that those who are experienced in fasting have a "clear and constant sense of their resources in God."[4] It is through God that we are sustained. As Jesus said, "I have food to eat that you know nothing about," referring to the nourishment of the Father (John 4:32). Foster mentions that fasting must be God prompted and God ordained. It is an act of obedience to the call of God.

Closely tied to this purpose, but secondary to centering on God, is that of self-denial. Fasting reveals how much we rely on the pleasure of eating for our contentment. We use food for comfort when we are feeling stressed, anxious, or afraid, even referring to some foods as "comfort foods." Fasting invites us to let go of this dependence and give it to God. Our belly is not our god but our servant. Eating is so pervasive in our lives that as we gain control over it, it affects all areas of our life. Willard says that as we fast, we learn moderation and constraint in regard to all our fundamental drives. We find contentment in the midst of all our desires.

As we deprive ourselves, struggles come to the surface—anger, pettiness, selfishness, feelings of worthlessness, jealousy, pride. We are no longer masking it with food or the endorphins that result from eating, so God has the opportunity to peel away the layers. This is a great grace as we recognize that Jesus is healing us through this process. Foster speaks of the freedom we receive as we achieve balance in our lives. He also mentions the additional benefits of "increased effectiveness in intercessory prayer, guidance in decisions, increased concentration, deliverance for those in bondage, physical well-being, and revelations."[5]

One word of caution: as with all forms of prayer, it is vital that we keep our eyes on Jesus rather than on ourselves. Again, the primary purpose is to center our lives on God. It is tempting to get too focused on the act of fasting or even the side-benefits or accolades from others and forget that this is for the purpose of giving ourselves more fully for God's use. As Jesus cautioned, "When you fast, do not look somber as the hypocrites do, for they disfigure their faces to show others they are fasting. Truly I tell you, they have received their reward in full. But when you fast, put oil on your head and wash your face, so that it will not be obvious to others that you are fasting, but only to your Father" (Matt. 6:16–18). Pairing the practice with prayer or service helps keep fasting from becoming too consuming—a god in itself.

My experience with fasting has been of the short-term variety— one to three days. I have found it to be a practice that allows for deep listening. It was helpful to me to think of it as feasting on God rather than deprivation. When my focus was on what I was doing without, it kept me at the center and detracted from a focus on God. However, when each pang of hunger became a trigger to turn my heart to God, it became a much more rewarding time of listening. On these one-day fasts, I have fasted in two ways: for twenty-four hours, missing three meals, and also for just two meals, skipping breakfast and lunch.

A three-day fast is more rewarding in terms of spiritual deepening. It allows movement beyond the first day, which I find the most difficult, when my body is rebelling against the abstinence. One beneficial strategy on this first difficult day is to find something to occupy myself with during regular mealtimes. I need this less after that initial day, as I can more easily devote myself to prayer during the time I would normally be eating. For me, the process highlights the offering I am making to God. Although certainly a meager gift, I revel in the opportunity to offer it.

Similar to longer times of silence, I develop a rhythm when fasting for more than one day. This rhythm occurs throughout the days of a fast and can be part of a more expansive pattern of ongoing fasting. A friend of mine has a rhythm of fasting one day each week. This began as a child when his father encouraged the whole family to fast together. It was a normal part of their family life and had tremendous spiritual benefits for him as he was growing up—especially as an adolescent. He now practices this rhythm with his own family and is seeing the same benefits in the lives of his children.

Each of the times I have fasted has involved a special purpose. It has accompanied either a difficult decision or a pleading for healing for a loved one. One such occasion was as a beloved relative was dying. It was a way of throwing myself at the feet of God to plead for the healing of my dear one. Although God did not grant my request, the comfort I received during that intense time with God sustained me through her death. Another instance was when I was faced with a career decision. Fasting was paired with silence and solitude as I sought to clear away the distractions in order to be attuned to God's guidance. Much of my dissonance was stripped away during the fasting, and I was able to see more clearly. This devoted time was followed with communal discernment as I sat with friends whom I respect for their deep love of God. Their questions, coupled with the clarity I had been given, was what I needed to move forward with the decision. Fasting was a significant component of that time. Not only was I able to make the decision, but the act itself was a physical means of communicating to myself and to God the weight of this decision.

I have not yet experienced a lengthy period of fasting. One friend recently went through an extended fast with her church. The leaders offer an invitation at the first of each year for anyone wanting to participate in a twenty-one-day fast. They support those fasting with daily devotional thoughts and a weekly gathering for encouragement and prayer. Her husband had participated the year previously, and she decided it was time to join him. Her hope was to be released from some toxic shame she had carried all her life.

The first week was very challenging. Foster talks about the body detoxing at the beginning, which is sometimes accompanied by a coated tongue and bad breath. The first three days are the most difficult due to the discomfort of hunger pain and having headaches from caffeine and sugar withdrawal. My friend spoke of being moody, irritable, and lacking energy. It was difficult to get beyond her hunger to the deeper intent. She thought constantly of wanting to eat. She said that prayer and gathering were vital as the community held each other accountable and encouraged each other. After the first week, it was much easier. She felt a clarity and energy. Although still hungry at times, she was more easily able to forget it. Her experience aligns with Foster, suggesting this is the most enjoyable part of the fast in terms of how one feels.

Sometime around the end of this second week, my friend said the shame she was trying to overcome came back in full force. She was tempted to avoid this pain but instead opened herself up to God's healing. This was a difficult time, a time of testing. She recognized she was moving into the space of letting go of control. She was surrendering the shame into God's hands. This struggle went on for a few days and then she felt released from it.

Throughout her whole fast, she experienced a "slowing." She said that emotions, typically overshadowed through distraction, were brought to the surface. Without the distraction of food, she sensed an ongoing choice to lean into herself and God or develop other forms of distraction. As she continually leaned into God, she was able to "just be." She said it felt as though time slowed, followed by her mind and body slowing. It was a time of resting—a time of being.

Those in biblical times fasted for forty days, and there is a physiological wisdom to this time frame. Anywhere between twenty-one and forty days, the hunger pains return, and the body begins the first stages of starvation.[6] It is important that the fast be ended at this time.

My friend said that her sense of shame returns from time to time, but the fast allowed for a significant shift in this struggle. She now knows she can trust God to control it. It is a matter of remembering.

PRACTICE

Praying Alone

This is the one prayer form that requires good physical health. It is important that a doctor is consulted before doing a lengthy fast. For the purposes of this book, we will focus on a short fast of one to three days.

- As you begin the fast, spend time dedicating your effort as an offering to God. Seek God's guidance and protection during the fast.
- Start small, perhaps skipping two meals. Drink juice or broth and plenty of water.
- Devote the time you would normally spend in meal prep, eating, and cleanup to God. Incorporate other contemplative prayer forms into this time.

- Commit to recognizing the hunger pangs as moments of God's healing as you are purified of toxins—physically and spiritually.
- You might commit to this practice once a week.
- After two or three weeks, increase your fast to a full day—missing three meals.
- Incorporate increased time in your day to journal about your experience—continually offering the dedicated time to God.
- Always break your fast gently with a small amount of fruit or vegetable juice.
- Maintain a posture of gratitude in this time of feasting on God.

Leading a Group

When leading a group in a fast, invite a firm commitment through prayer and discernment. An invitation can be made, but there should never be any pressure to participate. This is between the individual and God, not a requirement portraying spiritual maturity.

- If on retreat, a twenty-four-hour fast is appropriate for most. You can begin either after dinner or first thing in the morning.
- Gather together at the beginning of the day and assign each participant a partner.
- Give the following instructions:
  - "We are communing together in this time of abstinence from food. As we begin, take a deep breath and invite God to bring to your awareness a focus for your time of fasting. Breathe out any anxiety or concern you have about the fast or about addressing this focus.

> Breathe in God's love surrounding you and this intent. Take a couple of breaths like that."
>
> - "We're going to break into pairs, in order to spend time with your partner sharing the intent you want to bring to this focused time with God. Pray together and commit to holding each other in prayer during the fast."

- Allot about fifteen minutes for the time of prayer.
- Sound a chime to gather the entire group back together.
- Offer a prayer over the group, asking for God's protection and guidance.
- Tell them to come back together at the beginning of each regular mealtime for worship and encouragement.
- At the close of the fast, have the pairs meet again to share their experiences.
  - Sound a chime to bring the group back together to debrief as a body. Invite a few to share their experience.
  - To conclude, invite the participants one at a time to sit in the middle, with the group laying their hands on them.
  - Pray the following over each person: "God, you have begun something today of which only you know the extent. Bless (insert the name of the participant) with the courage and ability to continue on the path you have set before them. Amen."

Concluding Thoughts

Fasting is one of the most effective ways to attune to God. It allows for deep listening and has a significant impact on those who practice it regularly. As with other regular forms of contemplative prayer, it increases one's awareness of God's presence. And as with other efforts to be with God, we recognize that there are forces intent on discouraging us. Foster talks about fasting as being in the "realm of the Spirit."[7] We enter into the discipline in obedience to the prompt of the Spirit and trust that God communes with us there.

Additional Resources

Foster, Richard. *Celebration of Discipline: The Path to Spiritual Growth*, rev. ed. San Francisco: Harper & Row, 1988.

Thompson, Marjorie J. *Soul Feast: An Invitation to the Christian Spiritual Life*, rev. ed. Louisville: Westminster John Knox Press, 2014.

Willard, Dallas. *The Spirit of the Disciplines: Understanding How God Changes Lives*. New York: Harper & Row, 1988.

Notes

[1] Justo L. Gonzalez, *The Story of Christianity*, vol. 2 (New York: HarperCollins, 2010), 27.

[2] An in-depth history of the use of fasting can be found in John R. Tyson, ed., *Invitation to Christian Spirituality: An Ecumenical Anthology* (Oxford: Oxford University Press, 1999).

[3] Richard Foster, *Celebration of Discipline: The Path to Spiritual Growth*, rev. ed. (San Francisco: Harper & Row, 1988), 47.

[4] Dallas Willard, *The Spirit of the Disciplines: Understanding How God Changes Lives* (New York: HarperCollins, 1988), 167.

[5] Foster, *Celebration of Discipline*, 56.

[6] For more on the physiological impact of fasting, see Foster, *Celebration of Discipline*, 59.

[7] Foster, *Celebration of Discipline*, 60.

CHAPTER SEVEN

Walking the Labyrinth

The labyrinth is a path laid out in a circle on the ground. It is similar to a maze but with a specific path that leads to the center. One author writes, "[The Labyrinth] is a journey into an encounter with God in Jesus Christ."[1] It is a simple act of following a path that reaps significant blessing—an impact that increases the more one practices the discipline.

I do not recall the first time I walked a labyrinth. I have done so many times in various places through the years, most often in retreat centers. It has been one of my favorite means of prayer for years—so meaningful, in fact, that I had one built on our property. I never tire of the practice and am blessed each time I walk it. This walking prayer experience is always profound.

Background and History

In the early days of the church, believers would return to Jerusalem each year on a holy pilgrimage. It was a way to recommit to the

Lord—a time to confess one's sins and start anew. There were three movements that happened on the pilgrimage that coincided with the three stages of this journey. The first movement was purgation and occurred on the first stage as the pilgrims traveled to the Holy City. On the way, they considered their shortcomings and how they would like to be cleansed of these sins. It was a time of self-examination and confession—a time of taking responsibility and allowing oneself to truly see the manner in which they had strayed from the path.

This self-examination continued until the second stage of the journey—the arrival at Jerusalem. The second movement, illumination, then occurred. This was a time of fellowship, encouragement, and learning. Having admitted and released their wrongdoing, they were free to drink in the spiritual food of the Holy City. Refreshed, they then returned home—the final stage of the journey. They were now ready for the final movement: union. With full hearts, they were ready to enter into God's work in the world. As they traveled back to their regular lives, they offered themselves as instruments of the kingdom.

As the church grew and spread across the world, it became increasingly difficult for most Christians to make an annual journey to Jerusalem. They brought this dilemma to the church, and the leaders created a symbolic way for them to make the pilgrimage. This was the birth of the labyrinth—a representation of the holy pilgrimage. It was a journey with a clear path of twists and turns that led to a center. The pilgrim would journey to the center and then back out on the same path, just as they would on an actual pilgrimage. Author Bradley Holt states, "The labyrinth is not a maze, which confuses the searcher, but rather a very clear path from the periphery to the centre and back out again."[2]

As we walk the labyrinth, at times we find ourselves close to the center and then far away again. This happens repeatedly until, at last, we reach the sought-for destination. It offers a metaphor for many of the happenings of the Christian journey—the twists and turns, the hope of coming close but finding oneself far away again, the final arrival, and so on. Walking the labyrinth follows the same movements and stages of the pilgrimage on which it is based. The movements of purgation, illumination, and union coincide with walking in, being in the center, and walking out.

One of the most famous labyrinths is built into the floor of the Chartres Cathedral in France (see Figure 7.1). It is the pattern most often copied, although there are a number of other designs.

Figure 7.1: Chartres Cathedral Labyrinth

Much of my early experience with the labyrinth was at the retreat centers when I was on weekend silent retreats. The prayer form quickly became a favorite practice as I recognized the benefit of both the ritual and the movement. I love the idea of walking this sacred symbolic journey with saints throughout the ages. What might have been their experience walking the same path in the Middle Ages? What struggles did they bring to this prayer? And the kinesthetic aspect helped keep my thoughts centered on God. My mind tended to wander when I prayed, and walking the path gave structure to my thoughts.

It is a joy to lead others in this beloved prayer form. There are always a number of participants on a retreat who have never walked the labyrinth. Even though I tell them the path is longer than it seems, they are surprised at how long it takes. Yet, without exception, they find the experience meaningful and are eager to carve out time to walk it on their own. They and the rest of the group, albeit in silence, have a strong sense of the community in this shared journey. It draws them closer to each other as they draw closer to God.

PRACTICE

As mentioned previously, a surprising element of walking a labyrinth is the length of the path. It takes longer than initially anticipated. This time is important, as it, along with the cadence of the walk, allows you to move from your head to your heart and settle in to allow God to direct you.

Praying Alone

- Before you begin, pause and take a few deep breaths. This helps you let go of the many distractions of the mind and be present to the moment and the experience.
- Offer yourself to God and ask for guidance as you pray.

- The first movement, *purgation*, occurs as you walk toward the center.
  - Walk in a meditative manner—slow and steady. You will quickly develop a cadence as you find your stride.
  - As you walk, allow the Spirit to bring to your awareness the things that need to come to the surface. When faced with any intended or unintended sins, grudges, hurt, or anger, do your best to be open to whatever the Spirit brings. As these thoughts come to mind, give them to God. It can be helpful to visualize yourself handing them over to God.
  - If your mind wanders, focus on the path and your walking.
- *Illumination* is the movement that occurs when you reach the center.
  - Open yourself up to God. It can be helpful to lift your hands to God or kneel. You are opening yourself to whatever it is that God has for you.
  - It is important to remember that we do not control God. Thus we are not demanding insight or epiphany; we are opening ourselves to that possibility. God may choose to just be with us, and that is enough!
  - Stay for as long as you like. It may be a few minutes or even an hour. Some carry their journals and spend time recording their thoughts as they sit in the center.
- When you are ready, the movement of *union* begins as you step onto the path for the journey back out.
  - You might lift your eyes and recognize the beauty of God's creation around you.
  - Allow your mind to focus on the context of your everyday life.

- Offer yourself as an instrument for use in the kingdom. Again, don't try to control it—open yourself to what the Spirit may have for you. You may be given specific ideas or just rest in a sense of joy in being available for God's use.
- When you reach the opening and prepare to leave the labyrinth, pause and lift your arms to God, offering yourself in a prayer of dedication and availability.

Leading a Group

Walking the labyrinth as a group is a sweet time of community. You are not engaging with each other verbally, but the sense of spirit and communion is strong as you pray together.

- Gather the group near the opening of the labyrinth.
- Share the background and intent of the practice.
- Then give the following instructions:
  - "Walk in a meditative way—slow and steady."
  - "Honor the 'coveting of the eyes.' This means that we avoid eye contact with others in order to allow them to have their focused time with God."
  - "As you walk in, experience the movement of purgation as you let go of your sins and struggles."
  - "If someone before you is walking more slowly than you prefer, step off the path to pass them. Remember where you are on the path (in order to avoid becoming confused)."
  - "When you arrive at the center, stay for a few minutes. The experience as a group does not allow for too much time there, but you can come back later for a longer time. Experience illumination as you open yourself to whatever the Spirit has for you."

- ■ "As you walk back out, enter into the time of union with God as you offer yourself for God's use."
- ■ "In this stage, you will meet people still coming into the center, so just gently step off the path for a moment and let them pass. Again, remember where you are so as not to lose your place."
- ■ "When you arrive back at the opening, pause and lift your hands to God as a gesture of offering yourself for God's use."
- ■ "When you are finished, stand around the edge and pray for the others until the last person is finished."
- ■ "Leave in silence."
- • I will often encourage the participants to walk in silence back to our meeting space and then have a time of debriefing.

Experiencing the practice of walking the labyrinth in a group will often lead individuals to walk it on their own, as I shared earlier. Praying as individuals and with a group can be quite different. Both allow for deep communion with God.

Concluding Thoughts

I was once leading a group of faculty and university administrators in this practice. I shared the background and encouraged them to begin when they were ready. Someone asked me a question, and I momentarily shifted my focus away from what was happening on the labyrinth. Another person then tapped me on the shoulder and asked, "Is that person supposed to be doing that?" I looked up and saw one very driven person ignoring the path and walking straight to the center. I told him that he was actually supposed to follow the path, and he said, "But isn't the goal to get to the middle?"

It was a funny experience, and he was right. Part of the goal *is* to get to the center. However, "the joy is in the journey" is an appropriate phrase to bear in mind when walking the labyrinth. If it is entered with the belief that the sole "goal" is to get to the center, much will be missed. One may become frustrated with the amount of time it takes to get to the middle. It is the actual process of walking the labyrinth—the time on the path—that bears fruit. The prayer form is an apt metaphor for the life of a Christian. Each stage of the journey is equally important.

Additional Resources

Artress, Lauren. *Walking a Sacred Path: Rediscovering the Labyrinth as a Spiritual Practice*, rev. ed. New York: Riverhead Books, 2006.

Scholl, Travis. *Walking the Labyrinth: A Place to Pray and Seek God*. Downers Grove, IL: InterVarsity Press, 2014.

Notes

[1] Travis Scholl, *Walking the Labyrinth: A Place to Pray and Seek God* (Downers Grove, IL: InterVarsity Press, 2014), 17.

[2] Bradley P. Holt, "Spiritualities of the Twentieth Century," in *The Story of Christian Spirituality: Two Thousand Years from East to West*, ed. Gordon Mursell (Minneapolis: Fortress Press, 2001), 338.

CHAPTER EIGHT

Creation Prayer

Creation prayer is simply an openness to God's revelation to us through God's created world. Creation offers a significant means for encountering God. One of my earliest encounters with God occurred when I was a child around the age of ten. My family had recently moved from the prairies of Saskatchewan to the mountains of Montana. I loved the vast beauty of the prairies and was now enamored with the Rocky Mountains of our new home. We often spent time hiking, and one time, I remember we had hiked up a mountain and were spending a leisurely day in a mountain meadow. It was a beautiful day. The sky was a startling blue and the pine trees were the deep green of summer. I recall lying in the grass on my back amid the wildflowers and gazing up into the sky. The sun was warm on my face, and I could hear the bees buzzing lazily around me. My best descriptor of it is "delicious." The presence of God was palpable, and the love I felt for and from God was profound. This was the first time I was aware that my soul was being fed by the beauty of creation. What a gift!

I cannot count the times since that day in the mountain meadow that God has spoken to me through creation. The sense of awe I felt for God at the magnificence of the mountains has been matched by the majesty of the ocean and the still presence in a quiet forest. I have learned to seek out places of beauty for nourishment when my soul is dry. And God has expanded my understanding of splendor as my eyes have been opened to beauty that is unexpected, such as the sudden glory of a sunset or a wildflower that offers a stark contrast to the dullness of the surrounding landscape.

It thrills me to consider that beauty is a gift that God did not have to include in the world. I suppose that God could have been much more pragmatic in making the world, with little attention given to the aesthetic. But, thankfully, ours is an imaginative Creator God—an artist who created us in his own image. Creation feeds our souls.

We have only to open our eyes to see the wonder that surrounds us. We *need* this wonder of creation, but even more, we *need* the capacity to notice. God speaks to us through creation, and it is our responsibility to listen.

Background and History

Many texts in the Old Testament attest to God's revelation through creation. In the book of Job, God's response to Job highlights this revelation. "But now ask the beasts, and let them teach you; and the birds of the heavens, and let them tell you. Or speak to the earth, and let it teach you; and let the fish of the sea declare to you. Who among all these does not know that the hand of the LORD has done this, in whose hand is the life of every living thing, and the breath of all mankind?" (Job 12:7–10 NASB). The psalmist tells us,

"The heavens are telling of the glory of God; and their expanse is declaring the work of His hands. Day to day pours forth speech, and night to night reveals knowledge. There is no speech, nor are there words; their voice is not heard. Their line has gone out through all the earth, and their utterances to the end of the world" (Ps. 19:1–4 NASB). And the prophet Isaiah states, "The mountains and the hills will break forth into shouts of joy before you, and all the trees of the field will clap *their* hands" (Isa. 55:12 NASB). We also see evidence of God's revelation through creation in the New Testament. Paul tells the Romans, "For since the creation of the world His invisible attributes, His eternal power and divine nature, have been clearly seen, being understood through what has been made, so that they are without excuse" (Rom. 1:20 NASB).

In addition, the church has provided witnesses to the testimony of creation. Francis, one of the most well-known saints, recognized the role of creation in bringing glory to God. He is known for his special relationship with animals and the environment. Francis referred to the sun and moon as his sister and brother, and he had a special relationship with animals. One story is told of him walking down the road and coming upon a flock of feeding birds. He told his companions that he needed to stop and preach to the birds. As he preached, the birds ceased all activity and seemed to listen intently. They did not move until he released them when he was finished. Another time, he was said to have spoken with a wolf that was terrorizing a village. The wolf agreed to stop its assault in exchange for being fed. Many gardens attest to St. Francis as a lover of creation through statues of him holding out his bird-laden arms.

The testimony of sacred Scripture and the church enter into partnership with the wonder of the created world and universe. They bring glory to God and speak to us of God's creativity and majesty. We join with these in listening. The witnesses to God's glory are without number. We need only to attune our eyes and hearts to this revelation.

There are many ways through which we see and hear God through creation.

Praying Alone

Noticing. The first, as alluded to previously, is to open the eyes of our heart to creation. There is no end to the ways it can speak to us. Of course, the beauty and majesty of mountains and oceans are rich with the voice of God. However, it is not limited to the grand. One can look into the eyes of a child and relish the beauty that God has created. Or notice a flower growing up through the crack in a concrete slab. It's about noticing. And it's about connecting the dots. I notice and allow gratitude to well up inside me for the generosity of our God. I love wild birds and have many feeders, birdbaths, and birdhouses around my property. It is a joy to sit and watch them and become familiar with the variety of tendencies, calls, and preferences of these fellow creatures. When I remember to be open to creation, God teaches me.

Being still in creation. A second means of bearing witness to God's presence in creation is to intentionally withdraw and spend time therein. A good practice is to walk around until you find a place in which you can be comfortable and undisturbed for a time. I often do this when at a retreat center or in my yard. Take a sketch pad or journal to assist in capturing the thoughts and insights that God brings. When you find a spot, settle in and notice your surroundings. Offer a prayer of thanks to God, along with a request that God will open your heart to what he has for you. Sketching is a meaningful practice for me, as it allows me to home in on something—a flower, a tree, a leaf—and let go of everything else. (I find it more difficult with birds because they won't stay still! But I have been able to sketch small lizards and turtles as they sun themselves on the rocks.)

Being active while in creation. Another way is to be active—walk, run, cycle, kayak—and be intentional about noticing God's presence. Not only am I immersed in the creation around me, but I am celebrating the creation of my body as it moves. It's helpful to begin in the same way as previously mentioned by dedicating the time to God and asking for God to bring to your mind what God has for you. It is similar to taking a walk with a friend. I pour out my heart and listen as God speaks to me through the creation around me. I trust that the insights I receive are from the Spirit.

Leading a Group

There are also beautiful ways to celebrate and pay attention to creation as a group. The following is a prayer that I often lead when directing a retreat. It's called a creation walk.

- Print out seven copies of the days of creation.
- Designate individuals to read them. I typically choose people who are not always in the lead.
- Instruct the designated readers to take the group, or position the group, to look at something that fits with the day of creation they are reading. For example, on the first day, have the group look up to the light of the sky. On day three, when God created vegetation, lead the group to stand among the trees or enjoy a flower bed. On day six (the creation of man and animals), have the group form a circle and look at each other. Allow the individuals who are reading to make this choice.

- Tell readers that at the end of their reading, they will say "God is good," and the group will answer, "All the time." The next reader, then, is to wait a few moments (after the group responds with "All the time") and then start walking to the place on which they have decided for their text. They will need to keep track of the order of the days so they know when their day is coming and can be ready to take the lead.

Give the following instructions to the entire group at the beginning of the exercise:

- "We're going to do a creation walk to celebrate God's gift of creation."
- "I've chosen seven people—each will read one of the days of creation."
- "When it is their turn, we will follow them to a different place on the property." (Encourage them to keep the length of their walk fairly short.)
- "They'll then read the day of creation that has been assigned to them."
- "At the end of their reading, the individual will say, 'God is good,' and you (the group) will answer, 'All the time.'"
- "The next designated person (with the next day of creation) will then lead the group to a new spot."

The days are outlined as follows.

Creation Prayer

Genesis 1–2:2 (NRSV)

Reader #1

In the beginning when God created the heavens and the earth, the earth was a formless void and darkness covered the face of the deep, while a wind from God swept over the face of the waters. Then God said, "Let there be light"; and there was light. And God saw that the light was good; and God separated the light from the darkness. God called the light Day, and the darkness he called Night. And there was evening and there was morning, the first day.

God is good! (Group answers: All the time!)

Reader #2
And God said, "Let there be a dome in the midst of the waters, and let it separate the waters from the waters." So God made the dome and separated the waters that were under the dome from the waters that were above the dome. And it was so. God called the dome Sky. And there was evening and there was morning, the second day.

God is good! (Group answers: All the time!)

Reader #3
And God said, "Let the waters under the sky be gathered together into one place, and let the dry land appear." And it was so. God called the dry land Earth, and the waters that were gathered together he called Seas. And God saw that it was good. Then God said, "Let the earth put forth vegetation: plants yielding seed, and fruit trees of every kind on earth that bear fruit with the seed in it." And it was so. The earth brought forth vegetation: plants yielding seed of every kind, and trees of every kind bearing fruit with the seed in it. And God saw that it was good. And there was evening and there was morning, the third day.

God is good! (Group answers: All the time!)

Reader #4
And God said, "Let there be lights in the dome of the sky to separate the day from the night; and let them be for signs and for

seasons and for days and years, and let them be lights in the dome of the sky to give light upon the earth." And it was so. God made the two great lights—the greater light to rule the day and the lesser light to rule the night—and the stars. God set them in the dome of the sky to give light upon the earth, to rule over the day and over the night, and to separate the light from the darkness. And God saw that it was good. And there was evening and there was morning, the fourth day.

God is good! (Group answers: All the time!)

Reader #5

And God said, "Let the waters bring forth swarms of living creatures, and let birds fly above the earth across the dome of the sky." So God created the great sea monsters and every living creature that moves, of every kind, with which the waters swarm, and every winged bird of every kind. And God saw that it was good. God blessed them, saying, "Be fruitful and multiply and fill the waters in the seas, and let birds multiply on the earth." And there was evening and there was morning, the fifth day.

God is good! (Group answers: All the time!)

Reader #6

And God said, "Let the earth bring forth living creatures of every kind: cattle and creeping things and wild animals of the earth of every kind." And it was so. God made the wild animals of the earth of every kind, and the cattle of every kind, and everything that creeps upon the ground of every kind. And God saw that it was good.

Then God said, "Let us make humankind in our image, according to our likeness; and let them have dominion over the fish of the sea, and over the birds of the air, and over the cattle, and over all the wild animals of the earth, and over every creeping thing that creeps upon the earth."

So God created humankind in his image, in the image of God he created them; male and female he created them.

God blessed them, and God said to them, "Be fruitful and multiply, and fill the earth and subdue it; and have dominion over the fish of the sea and over the birds of the air and over every living thing that moves upon the earth." God said, "See, I have given you every plant yielding seed that is upon the face of all the earth, and every tree with seed in its fruit; you shall have them for food. And to every beast of the earth, and to every bird of the air, and to everything that creeps on the earth, everything that has the breath of life, I have given every green plant for food." And it was so. God saw everything that he had made, and indeed, it was very good. And there was evening and there was morning, the sixth day.

God is good! (Group answers: All the time!)

Reader #7

Thus the heavens and the earth were finished, and all their multitude. And on the seventh day God finished the work that he had done, and he rested on the seventh day from all the work that he had done. So God blessed the seventh day and hallowed it, because on it God rested from all the work that he had done in creation.

God is good! (Group answers: All the time!)

Concluding Thoughts

God's revelation through creation surrounds us. We are met with it every moment of the day and yet, at times, our senses are closed to its teaching. The invitation offered to us is to open ourselves to the richness of this communication. We gain attunement to God's presence as we enter into this form of prayer.

CHAPTER NINE

Anglican Prayer Beads
(Protestant Prayer Beads
or Anglican Rosary)

I once confided to a friend that I was having difficulty stilling my mind when I prayed. This has been a lifelong issue for me. I have seasons when I am able to settle in quickly and maintain my focus on God. Yet, at times, I am not able to be present to God, despite all attempts through my willpower. My friend and I were at a residency for a training on leading contemplative prayer groups and retreats. This particular friend was one of the staff for the training, and one afternoon, we went for a walk. I told him of my love for contemplative prayer. It was a coming home for me—a way of being with God that I had experienced organically but had no words for before this program. Although I loved this listening side of prayer, I found it difficult to be present in the moment. The minute I settled in, my mind started racing—going over my list for the day, considering a difficulty at work, thinking about what was coming up—there was no end to the directions it was going. The harder I tried to focus on these occasions, the more my thoughts took off.

My friend told me this was often called "monkey mind" and reassured me that it was "normal." He went on to explain that those who are more extroverted (like himself) had difficulty getting to prayer, but once they were there, they could typically settle in. The challenge for those who are introverted (like me) is different. We are easily able to draw apart to be with God, but as we're used to being in our heads, the greatest battle is stilling our minds. He said there are a number of ways to address this struggle and suggested I add to my repertoire prayers that were kinesthetic in nature. These would help direct my focus.

After the residency, he sent me my first set of Anglican prayer beads. The gift was greater than he knew, as it not only initiated a love for this simple practice but helped me recognize my strong tendency toward the kinesthetic. As suggested by my friend, having something tactile with which to pray assists in being present in prayer. Praying with beads was a foreign concept to me—perhaps tied in my subconscious to a fear, passed on to me in my faith background, of idolatry. Since the receipt of those beads, however, I have had numerous sets of prayer beads. Not only do I pray with them myself; I have given many as gifts and led groups in praying with them and even in creating them as a practice in prayer. I now pray on a daily basis with a set I made many years ago. The exercise continues to be a rich avenue to communion with God as it connects my mind, body, and heart.

Background and History

The practice of praying with beads dates back thousands of years and has been used by every major faith tradition. The Catholic rosary is the most familiar use of this method. The desert mothers and fathers of the third century encouraged the practice of dropping pebbles for each prayer or tying knots into a string as a way to engage the body in the exercise of prayer. In the ninth century, the Irish community of St. Columba began using colorful beads to replace the knots. Estes tells us that the origin of the word *bead* actually comes from the Anglo-Saxon word *bebe*, which means "to pray or request."[1]

In the early days of monasticism, the monks had rosaries of 150 beads for use in praying the Psalms—one bead for each chapter. This practice was daunting for the illiterate in the church, so in order to accommodate them, the use of a shorter prayer, the Lord's Prayer, was implemented instead. When Martin Luther broke from the Catholic church, he continued to pray with the rosary and encouraged its use. However, it eventually diminished in use by the Protestant church. In the 1980s, a prayer group of Episcopalians led by Rev. Lynn Bauman resurrected the practice and adapted it for Protestant use.[2] They included thirty-three beads to represent the years of the life of Jesus. This includes four large beads, called *cruciform beads*, to represent the cross; twenty-eight smaller beads (four sets of seven), called *weeks*; and one invitatory bead (see Figure 9.1). There are several symbolisms within the structure of the beads. First, the beads form a circle when laid out, and the four cruciform beads form a cross to emphasize the centrality of the cross to our faith. Second, the seven beads in each week represent the days of the week, the days of creation, and the seven seasons of the church. Next, the invitatory bead suggests an entrée into praise and worship. Finally, the practice begins with the cross and ends with the cross—again representing the centrality of the cross in our lives.

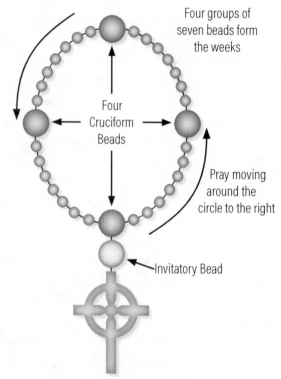

Figure 9.1: Episcopalian Rosary

I invite you to try this favorite prayer of mine. It is a calming, centering practice for me as I light my candle, pick up my beads, and pray through them each morning as part of my devotions.

PRACTICE

Praying Alone
Sit in a quiet, comfortable location that is free from distractions.

- Light a candle to represent the presence of the Spirit.
- Settle yourself in a comfortable position and hold the beads in your lap.

- Grasp the beads lightly between your thumb and forefinger as you follow them around the circle.
- Begin with the assigned prayer for the cross and then the invitatory bead, and then follow the beads to the right.
- The typical practice is to enter the circle and then go around the beads (the cruciform and weeks) three times in a slow, meditative manner.
- After the third time, go back to the invitatory bead and then exit with the cross. You can, of course, go around fewer or more times.

The repetition takes you from your head to your heart as you let go of thinking and focus on the prayers. The tactile aspect keeps your mind from wandering. It also allows you to close your eyes and let your fingers walk around the circle.

Another option is to pray with them as you walk or drive. You do not need to see them, as the varying sizes and shapes allow you to pray without looking at them. The following are two examples that use traditional prayers of the church with the beads.

The first example incorporates the prayers of Julian of Norwich, considered one of the greatest English theologians and Christian mystics. She is one of my heroes of faith. Although her writings received sparse attention during her time, they are now widely popular. Little is known about her other than her writings regarding the sixteen visions she received in 1373 during a time of mortal illness. She recovered and spent the remainder of her life as an anchoress, a holy solitary, of the church. She isolated herself in a monastic cell attached to the parish church, where she spent her time writing and receiving visitors who came for spiritual direction. Her main conclusion from her meditation is captured in a portion of the last chapter of her writing:

And from the time it was revealed, I desired many times to know in what was our Lord's meaning. And fifteen years after and more, I was answered in spiritual understanding, and it was said, "What, do you wish to know your Lord's meaning in this thing? Know it well, love was his meaning. Who reveals it to you? Love. What did it reveal to you? Love. Why does he reveal it to you? For love."[3]

We thus see the essence of what was revealed to her in her visions was that love, not judgment and anger, is the character of God. We see this in her prayers (set in *italics*) in the following outline for praying with Anglican prayer beads.

Julian of Norwich Prayer

The Cross
In the Name of God, Father, Son, and Holy Spirit. Amen.

The Invitatory
O God make speed to save me (us).
O Lord make haste to help me (us).
Glory to the Father, and to the Son, and to the Holy Spirit,
As it was in the beginning, is now, and will be forever.
Amen.

The Cruciforms (Say this full prayer on each cruciform bead.)
God of your goodness, give me yourself,
For you are enough to me.
And I can ask for nothing less that is to your glory.
And if I ask for anything less, I shall still be in want, for only in
*   you have I all.*

The Weeks (Pray on each bead.)
All shall be well, and all shall be well,
And all manner of things shall be well.
Or
In His love He has done His works, and in His love He has made
all things beneficial to us.

The Invitatory (Pray on exiting.)
The Lord's Prayer

The Cross (Pray on exiting.)
I bless the Lord (or we bless the Lord),
Thanks be to God.[4]

The second example includes prayers from Celtic spirituality or, more specifically, medieval Irish spirituality. The spirituality of Ireland at this time was closely connected to the natural and social environment. It was not part of the Roman Empire and thus was not organized by cities or roads like its neighboring countries. It was a wild landscape with the social system organized around tribes and local kings, resulting in indigenous forms of church organization and spirituality.[5]

Celtic spirituality is most widely known for a connection to nature. They regarded nature as a mirror of God's glory. This love of nature is apparent in the following poem from the ninth century:

A hedge of trees surrounds me,
A blackbird's voice sings to me;
Above my lined book
The call of birds chants to me.

In a grey mantle from the topmost bush
The cuckoo sings;
Truly may the good Lord protect me;

At peace I shall write under the green canopy.[6]

Another emphasis of this ancient Christian spirituality is on the community and the spiritual needs of each member. The practice of spiritual direction or *anam chara*, soul friend, had its beginning in this context as mature Christians offered spiritual guidance to those new in the faith. A saying attributed to monastic leader St. Brigid was "A person without a soul friend is a body without a head."

A prayer that is considered to be from the tradition of Gaelic spirituality, another name for Celtic spirituality, and thought to be passed from one soul friend to another is as follows:

> I weave a silence on my lips.
> I weave a silence into my mind.
> I weave a silence within my heart.
> I close my ears to distractions.
> I close my eyes to attentions.
> I close my heart to temptations.
>
> Calm me, O Lord, as you stilled the storm.
> Still me, O Lord, keep me from harm.
> Let all the tumult within me cease.
> Enfold me, Lord, in your peace.[7]

This is considered by some to be chanted by Celtic women in preparation for prayer. I find this to be a lovely practice and have a copy of it hanging on my wall. It reminds me of the sacredness inherent in the act of prayer. The opportunity to come before the Lord is not to be taken lightly.

Celtic spirituality has made a resurgence and is popular in contemporary Christian circles. Many make a pilgrimage to some of the ancient monastic communities, such as Iona Abbey and Lindisfarne. The prayers in the following format for the Anglican prayer beads come from *Carmina Gadelica*, a compilation of traditional rhymes, prayers, blessings, and songs gathered in the Gaelic-speaking regions by Alexander Carmichael in the nineteenth century.[8]

A Celtic Prayer

The Cross
In the Name of God, Father, Son, and Holy Spirit. Amen.

The Invitatory
O God made speed to save me (us).
O Lord make haste to help me (us).
Glory to the Father, and to the Son, and to the Holy Spirit,
As it was in the beginning, is now, and will be forever.
Amen.

The Cruciforms (Say this full prayer on each cruciform bead.)
Be the eye of God dwelling with me,
The foot of Christ in guidance with me,
The shower of the Spirit pouring on me,
Richly and generously.

The Weeks (Pray each phrase on a separate bead.)
I bow before the Father who made me,
I bow before the Son who saved me,
I bow before the Spirit who guides me,
In love and adoration.
I praise the Name of the one on high.
I bow before thee, Sacred Three,
The ever One, the Trinity.

The Invitatory (Pray on exiting.)
The Lord's Prayer

The Cross (Pray on exiting.)
I bless the Lord (or we bless the Lord),
Thanks be to God.[9]

Other methods for praying alone:

- Any prayer can be substituted for both the cruciform and
  the weeks. I also use the "Prayer of Abandonment" by
  Charles de Foucauld. He was known for the practice of a
  contemplative hospitable presence among and on behalf
  of his neighbors. He dedicated his life to living and working among the nomadic people of Algiers—eventually
  being killed by Bedouin tribesmen during a revolt against
  French colonial power. His prayer portrays his powerful
  devotion to Christ:

  Father,
  I abandon myself into your hands; do with me what
  you will.
  Whatever you may do, I thank you:
  I am ready for all, I accept all.
  Let only your will be done in me, and in all
  your creatures.
  I wish no more than this, O Lord.

  Into your hands I commend my soul;
  I offer it to you
  with all the love of my heart,
  for I love you, Lord,
  and so need to give myself,
  to surrender myself into your hands,
  without reserve,
  and with boundless confidence,
  for you are my Father.[10]

- One can also use the verses of a psalm, such as Psalm 23. Each phrase can be prayed on a different bead.
- Another use is in the practice of intercessory prayer— praying for a different person on each bead.

If possible, allow time to journal following the time of prayer with the beads.

Concluding Thoughts

There is no limit to the prayer that can be used with the beads. The important aspects are the repetition that becomes a cadence and drops you from your head to your heart. After using the Anglican prayer beads for a time, you will find that the beads help you settle in quickly to the stillness as they become an anchor to relax your body, mind, and heart.[11]

Additional Resources

Estes, Jenny Lynn. *The Anglican Rosary*. Bakersfield, CA: Theophany Press, 2019.

Evans, Jean West. "Your Anglican Prayer Beads." Pamphlet, 2001.

Notes

[1] Jenny Lynn Estes, *The Anglican Rosary* (Bakersfield, CA: Theophany Press, 2019), 6.

[2] Estes, *The Anglican Rosary*, 6.

[3] Bernard McGinn, *The Essential Writings of Christian Mysticism* (New York: Modern Library, 2006), 238.

[4] Jean West Evans, "Your Anglican Prayer Beads."

[5] Philip Sheldrake, *Spirituality: A Brief History*, 2nd ed. (Chichester, West Sussex: Wiley-Blackwell, 2013), 68.

[6] Gordon Mursell, *The Story of Christian Spirituality: Two Thousand Years, from East to West* (Minneapolis: Fortress Press, 2001), 78.

[7] David Adam, *The Edge of Glory: Prayers in the Celtic Tradition* (London: SPCK Publishing, 2011).

[8] Alexander Carmichael, *Carmina Gadelica: Hymns and Incantations with Illustrative Notes on Words, Rites, and Customs, Dying and Obsolete* (Sydney: Wentworth Press, 2019).

[9] Evans, "Your Anglican Prayer Beads."

[10] Charles de Foucauld, *Charles de Foucauld*, Modern Spiritual Masters (Maryknoll, NY: Orbis Books, 1996), 104.

[11] Estes, *The Anglican Rosary*, 6.

CHAPTER TEN

Journaling Prayer

Journaling prayer is a prayer form in which one writes a letter to God and then records God's response. In my daily prayer, I use this form not every day but often. On retreat, however, it is a constant. It offers me the opportunity to pour myself out to God and listen to God's response. It is another kinesthetic practice that helps to focus my mind in prayer. The act of writing keeps my attention on interaction with God.

I also include journaling prayer in every retreat I lead. Anecdotally, it seems to be the most impactful form I teach. The participants frequently approach it with skepticism, only to be surprised at the outcome. The latter part, recording God's response, is the part that initially invites skepticism.

Background and History

I do not know the origin of this form of prayer. It is a lovely practice that gives credence to the listening side of prayer. A quotation attributed to Martin Luther states, "If the Holy Spirit should come when these thoughts are in your mind and begin to preach to your heart, giving you rich and enlightened thoughts, then give Him the honor; let your preconceived ideas go, be quiet and listen to Him who can talk better than you; and note what He proclaims and *write it down*."

Journaling a two-way conversation with God is beautiful in its simplicity and profound in the truth of God's active presence in our lives. The conversation, of course, has two parts. The first part, writing a letter to God, is familiar to many. It is rare to find an individual who has not journaled a prayer on their own or as part of a retreat or class on spiritual formation. We take our cue from the Psalms as we see both praise and lament being poured out to God on the pages of the text.

The second part, God's response, is the part of the conversation that takes participants by surprise. There are often expressions that it feels disrespectful or arrogant to assume one knows the words with which God would respond. This is, of course, true. We have no right to put words in God's mouth. However, when one lets go of their concerns and opens up to the experience, the words typically pour forth onto the page. We have a history with God—both through Scripture and through our life experiences and other modes of revelation through which God communicates. We develop the ability to listen to the promptings of the Spirit and invitations of our Father. Thus it is not about putting words in the mouth of God but about living in the reality that God is present and active in our lives. God did not set the world in motion and leave us to our own devices but is *alive*! The psalmist states, "Be still and know that I am God" (Ps. 46:10).

Author Mark Virkler bases his practice of two-way journaling on a study of Habakkuk 2. He encourages going to a silent place and opening ourselves to whatever manner God may choose to communicate with us. I appreciate his description of recognizing God speaking to us as follows: "[H]earing God's voice is recognizing that God's voice in your heart often sounds like a flow of spontaneous thoughts."[1] This way of articulating it is akin to the words of Martin Luther: "Holy Spirit . . . [will] begin to preach to your heart, giving you rich and enlightened thoughts."[2]

I have journal after journal filled with this form of prayer. It is a rich companion when on retreat because I am free of the distractions that capture my attention. In this set-aside time, I have the opportunity to listen intently and to record God's communication. I typically set out for a walk after breakfast. I keep an eye out for a good spot, and when I find it, I settle in with my journal. I sit quietly for a while and let my thoughts go where they will. I then pray with a passage of Scripture and again allow my mind to wander. When I feel ready, I begin writing my prayer and let it flow out of me. After a time, I stop and listen to what is welling up in my soul. The act of writing it in my journal solidifies my thoughts (while also giving me a wonderful record of this interaction).

Sometimes I am surprised by what I hear from God. The words just flow out onto the page almost faster than my mind can even process. But most often, I am not surprised. Familiar messages emerge, such as "I love you without condition" or "Let go, my child; let me carry that for you." The timing is impeccable as I recognize how hungry I've been for God's guidance.

PRACTICE

This practice is a two-way conversation with God.

Praying Alone

- Settle into a comfortable space, free from distractions. As stated previously, I often go outside to allow creation to be part of the experience, but a snug chair is good as well.

- Have an adequate amount of paper—more than you need. You do not want to interrupt your prayer to find additional materials. I choose a good pen that flows well. (This is not entirely necessary—I am picky about my pens!)

- A good amount of time for the experience is twenty minutes—ten for each part. Set a timer for each ten-minute segment so you do not have to check the time. This allows you to give yourself fully to the prayer. When you have gained experience with the prayer form, a timer will not be needed. You will switch when you feel ready.

- As you begin, breathe in God's love and breathe out any concerns or darkness you are holding. Offer yourself and this prayer into God's keeping. Ask that you be open to whatever God has for you.

- For the first portion, start the timer and begin with the words "Dear God" or "My dear Father"—a name/relationship with which you are comfortable.

- Then let your thoughts pour out onto the page. Don't control it; just let it flow. You might have a lot to say or just a short amount. Don't judge what you write—anything is appropriate.

- When the ten minutes are up, set the timer for the next ten and begin writing God's response.

- Again, begin with something endearing, such as "My dear daughter," "My dear child," "Dear Jackie."

- Then let God's response flow out in your words. Again, don't try to control it. Don't even try to answer what you wrote earlier—just let it pour out. It may be long or short.

- When the timer sounds, spend a few moments resting in God's presence.

Sometimes the words tumble out and the ten minutes is not enough. At other times, you may write a short amount for your part or God's part and it feels right. Again, try your best not to control it.

One time when I was leading a retreat, a participant said that all he could write was "I am not worthy." He then told me, as his eyes welled up with tears, that God's response was short as well—"I love you!" That was exactly what he needed to hear—no convincing, no list of how God loved him. This friend just needed God's loving affirmation. As happens to me, you will find that you are not really surprised at the response you receive from God. It is loving—sometimes a gentle chiding, but always loving.

Leading a Group
Explain the prayer as follows:

- "We are going to do a journaling prayer. The first part will be familiar to you—we will write a letter to God. The second part is unexpected to many, as we will allow God to respond. Let go of your skepticism and just participate. The experience of the prayer may surprise you. We have a history with God, and that relationship tends to flow through as we write God's response."
- "I will keep a timer, and we will spend ten minutes on each part. At the end of the first ten minutes, you'll hear the chime and know it is time to begin God's response."
- "You are welcome to keep your own time if you want to go outside or into another part of the building. Just be back in twenty minutes."
- Hand out paper and pens or pencils.
- Continue with the following instructions:
  - "Put everything down but your paper and pen."

117

- ▪ "Breathe in God's love and light, filling yourself with God's love. Breathe out any worries or concerns you are holding about home, work, or relationships. Breathe in again God's love and light—let it flow through every part of you. Breathe out any darkness or sadness. Take a couple of breaths like that."
- ▪ "For the first part, pour out your heart onto the paper in your letter to God. Just let it flow; don't control it. It might be a lot or a little; it doesn't matter."
- ▪ "I'll sound the chime at the end of the first part, for those of you who are staying in this room."
- ▪ "For the second part, begin with a term of endearment, such as 'My dear child' or 'My loved one' or your name."
- ▪ "Then, again, just let it flow. It may be a lot or a little. Try not to control it. Don't even try to respond to what you wrote earlier."

- Allow a few minutes for people to leave the room and then begin the timer. Sound the chime at ten minutes.
- Continue the instructions:
  - ▪ "Remember to begin the second part with a term of endearment, such as 'My dear child' or 'My loved one' or your name."
  - ▪ "Then just let it flow. Try not to control it."

- When the timer sounds, sound the chime and take a few minutes to allow the group to reassemble.
- Say the following:
  - ▪ "We're now going to have a time of sharing. What you wrote is between you and God, but we will share about the process. Do not share anything that makes you uncomfortable."

- ▪ "Turn to the person next to you and share your experience."

- Allow the sharing to continue for a few minutes.
- Then invite sharing with the larger group as follows:
  - ▪ "Is there anyone who would like to share with the larger group? Again, what you wrote is between you and God. Share about the experience."

Concluding Thoughts

I have been leading retreats for many years and have found that every single participant I've encountered has been blessed by this experience. It has had a profound impact on some—many of whom were skeptical at the beginning of the prayer. They often decide to incorporate prayer journaling into their regular prayer practice.

Notes

[1] Mark Virkler and Patti Virkler, *Four Keys to Hearing God's Voice* (Shippensburg, PA: Destiny Image Publishers, 2010), 96.

[2] J. I. Packer and Carolyn Nystrom, *Praying: Finding Our Way through Duty to Delight* (Downers Grove, IL: InterVarsity Press, 2006), 288.

CHAPTER ELEVEN

Art as Prayer

Art is a vital form of prayer that offers both a means and an outcome with which to pray. It is another way that the body, soul, and heart are brought together in prayer.

In her course on art and spirituality, Susan Ernst talks about art as a vehicle through which we can be authentic. It allows us to express both positive and negative emotions. One example is the way that color both affects our moods and reflects our moods. She cites how we use color in our language—"I feel blue" or "life is rosy." Another example of authenticity in art is expression through song or story. "Songs can be joyful or mournful, and great stories and poetry lift our spirits or move us to tears." We use art to face pain and sadness with integrity—and as we express ourselves, beauty pours forth.[1]

The willingness to be vulnerable, to allow the ugliness to show, is powerful. The honesty touches our hearts and the hearts of those who experience our art, and we are moved. If we ignore the pain and project only happiness, our resulting expression is shallow.

What a beautiful description of prayer! When created with the intent to engage with God, both the artistic process and product become prayer. Visual arts, poetry, music, dramatic arts—all can become ways in which we converse with God. We pour out our emotions and receive healing as God speaks to us through the art. It does not require expertise—simply a willingness to engage with God in this manner.

In her book entitled *Walking on Water: Reflections on Faith and Art*, Madeleine L'Engle states, "God is constantly creating, in us, with us, through us, and to co-create with God is our human calling."[2] It is the willingness or obedience to create that is important. She uses the annunciation of Mary to illustrate her point. When Mary was approached by the angel, she responded with humble, courageous obedience. L'Engle says, "[E]ach work of art, whether it is a work of great genius or something very small, comes to the artist and says, 'Here I am. Enflesh me. Give birth to me.' And the artist either says, 'My soul doth magnify the Lord,' and willingly becomes the bearer of the work, or refuses."[3]

For the purposes of this discussion on art as prayer, we recognize the importance of a listening, open stance to God. The focus is removed from us—whether we are doing it right and our qualifications—as we allow God to work through us with whatever creativity and ability we offer for his use.

Background and History

Art as prayer is a broad topic! From the beginning of time, humans have expressed their devotion and despair to God through art. There is no time in the history of the world that is devoid of the expression of the divine. And throughout the centuries, the church has utilized art to communicate and invite people into the story of

God. The early church avoided expressing their faith in art due to its Jewish roots and a strong prohibition against idolatry. It was not too long, however, before Christians were expressing the Christian story through various media, such as pictorial art (prints, paintings, books, manuscripts), architecture, sculptures, and applied arts (metalwork and textiles). Art historian Beth Williamson mentions that the existence of Christian art offers a distinction from the Jewish faith.[4] She goes on to state that for the believer, the historical purpose of religious art was primarily personal devotion. For the church, it served many purposes—theological and political, for instance. By the ninth century, Christian art was embedded in the doctrine and worship of the church.

Writer Jaroslav Pelikan offers an interesting study of Christian art and representations of Jesus throughout the centuries. The one thing these various artists have in common is their reverence for the person of Jesus Christ. Pelikan states, "For each age the life and teachings of Jesus presented an answer (or more often, *the* answer) to the most fundamental questions of human existence and of human identity." These depictions give us a window into the characteristics of the age. The artists, in essence, created Christ in their own likeness. Their thoughts, joy, and pain are incorporated into their representations of Christ.[5]

Another emphasis in the recognition of art as prayer is that Christian art is not necessarily religious art. L'Engle highlights the false dichotomy between the secular and religious. She states that rather than polarization, artists who truly listen to God begin to recognize that the sacred is all around them. Although some still hold onto the dichotomy and fight over what is acceptable to represent in art, others "have left the war and put their energy instead into doing their work with as much excellence as they can, living their faith with as much honesty and humility as they can muster, and embracing mystery with as much passion as possible."[6]

What a lovely description of art as prayer. We seek excellence, honesty, and humility as we become open to God creating in us, with us, and through us. We embrace the mystery with passion.

PRACTICE

There are, of course, unlimited means of artistic expression that can be utilized as prayer. Here I will limit my instructions to a few simple forms.

Praying Alone

To begin, dedicate your time to God and ask that God help you be open to what message he has for you in this time of prayer. Make sure you have your supplies within reach to allow for an undisturbed time with God.

- Sketching
  - There are a variety of supplies that can be used with sketching. I use my regular journal and a black pen. A pencil set, eraser, and sketch pad are also good—especially if this is a regular means of prayer.
  - One method is to go on a walk with eyes that are attuned to the beauty of creation. Allow something to "grab" your attention and let that become your subject.
  - Settle in and again offer the time to God. Lose yourself in the sketching of the object. I often choose a flower, leaf, tree, or pinecone—something that is easily accessible.
  - Sometimes I'll take a photo of a bird or animal and sketch it from my phone.
  - It is important to enjoy the process and let go of the need to "do it right." The point is to immerse oneself in something of beauty that God has created.

- Another method is to settle into a comfortable spot inside and sketch a plant or a photo. The important thing is to come to the process with a heart of gratitude for the art of God.

- Photography
  - In a way that is similar to the sketching exercise, offer time to God and open the eyes of your heart as you walk around.
  - Allow yourself to see through a lens that captures the many forms of God's creativity in nature.
  - Spend time in *Visio Divina* (or "divine seeing") with your photos, allowing various aspects to emerge as you open yourself to the Spirit.
  - If leading a group, give each participant a disposable camera and then develop the photos at a venue with one-hour development. Individuals can spend time gazing at their own photos, or the group can share and pray with all of them.

- *Visio Divina* with images
  - Choose an image in a catalog, website, or museum. (It can be religious but doesn't need to be.)
  - Look at the image and allow your eyes to stay with the first thing you notice.
  - Gaze at it for a minute or so.
  - Then pull your vision back and take in the entire image for another minute or so.
  - What emotions does this bring up? What prayer rises within you?
  - Write the prayer(s) in your journal.
  - Offer your prayer(s) to God.

- Coloring
    - There are many available forms of adult coloring books. Many have themes of creation, patterns, or mandalas.
    - The point is to lose yourself in the creative activity and offer the time to God. Open yourself to whatever insights may come and find joy in the process.
    - Journal these insights.

- Personal psalm
    - Decide the number of lines you want to include—eight is a good starting number.
    - For the first portion (four lines), pour out your distress to God. Don't hold back or soften it.
    - For the second portion, begin with "Even so . . . ," and write four lines of praise.
    - The lines of praise can be connected to your distress or may be seemingly unrelated.
    - As you become more comfortable, write more lines and experiment with writing them in different ways.

Leading a Group

When leading a group, you can use the previously noted forms of art or other methods, such as collaging or simple calligraphy. Ensure the following:

- Know your chosen medium well enough to explain it and assist the participants if they need help.
- Have all the necessary supplies.
- Make sure it will be easy to transport—especially for participants traveling by plane.
- Explain the art, making the connection to God. This bridge can be lost in the scramble to get everyone set up.

- When you are all finished or later in the retreat (if the art needs time to dry), bring the group together for a "show and tell."
- Give the following instructions:
  - "Each participant will share their finished piece."
  - "As you share, include how God was working through you in both the process and the finished product."

Concluding Thoughts

One of the serendipities of this form of prayer is the ongoing blessing of the completed project. It becomes something of an icon that takes you immediately back to this prayerful experience of co-creation with God.

Additional References

Ernst, Susan. "Art and Spirituality: Lesson Six: Living an Artful Life." 2017. www.selahspiritual.com/art-and-spirituality/.

L'Engle, Madeleine. *Walking on Water: Reflections on Faith and Art.* New York: Crown Publishing, 2001.

Pelikan, Jaroslav. *Jesus through the Centuries: His Place in the History of Culture.* New Haven, CT: Yale University Press, 1985.

Williamson, Beth. *Christian Art: A Very Short Introduction.* New York: Oxford University Press, 2004.

Notes

[1] Susan Ernst, "Art and Spirituality: Lesson Six: Living an Artful Life," 2017, www.selahspiritual.com/art-and-spirituality/.

[2] Madeleine L'Engle, *Walking on Water: Reflections on Faith and Art* (New York: Crown Publishing, 2001), xv.

[3] L'Engle, *Walking on Water*, 8.

[4] Beth Williamson, *Christian Art: A Very Short Introduction* (New York: Oxford University Press, 2004), line 286.

[5] Jaroslav Pelikan, *Jesus through the Centuries: His Place in the History of Culture* (New Haven, CT: Yale University Press, 1985), 6.

[6] L'Engle, *Walking on Water*, xv.

OTHER PRAYERS OF THE CHURCH

This final section includes prayers that, in a way similar to those in the previous sections, come from across the ages of the church. Their origins range from the early centuries of the church to within the last century.

Some of these forms of contemplative prayer, such as the process of examen and practicing the presence of God, are tied to a specific individual. Others are not tied to any one person but arose during a certain season of the church and have survived the test of time—prayers such as the Jesus Prayer and praying with icons. All have played a significant role in my life and in the lives of those who have practiced them throughout history.

CHAPTER TWELVE

Iconography

Icons are painted images of religious figures on wood that are used in devotion. They most often include Christ or the saints and are a flat representation of these figures.

My first exposure to icons was while I was participating in training to become a spiritual director. During one of our sessions, the entire group of thirty was led in the process of "praying with" an icon. It was projected onto a screen, and we were encouraged to "gaze" at the image. The particular icon we used, known as the *Christ Pantocrator*, dated back to the sixth or seventh century AD. It was the face of Christ; one side was perfect (representing his divinity) and the other was slightly disfigured (signifying his humanity).

I was skeptical of the validity of this practice. Although my thoughts were not fully formed, I realized later that I had some bias that the veneration of the image was a form of idolatry. Despite my doubt, however, I decided during this session to let go of my cynicism and enter fully into the prayer. I could not have been more surprised by the impact.

The perfect side of Christ's face was appealing to me. I had a sense that it represented the good and unspoiled aspects of my life. I wanted to keep my focus on that side. However, as I continued to gaze, my focus kept being drawn to the flawed side. At the time, I was experiencing some difficult challenges in my work. I had pleaded with God to release me from the situation, but no relief had come. As my gaze was held by the flawed side, I sensed the Spirit encourage me to let go of the desire to have a perfect life and embrace the difficulty of my life. That time with the icon opened up a well of pain within me. I was able to face it and recognize a sense of unity with the suffering Christ. His life was not easy, and yet he continued to move forward in obedience. Praying with the icon ushered in a shift in my perspective regarding my demand to live a pain-free life.

Background and History

The term *icon* comes from a Greek word meaning "image." These depictions of Christ and the saints were used for both educational purposes and worship. They initially gave visual expression to Christian beliefs in a world where few had the ability to read. Historian Justo Gonzalez states that a doctor of the church said, "If people ask me what I believe, I show them the inside of my church."[1] In the Eastern Church, the walls of the sanctuary are covered in these images. The icons are venerated because of a belief that they give one access to the sacred persons that they represent. In this way, icons are windows into another world—revelations into heaven. During the eighth and ninth centuries, controversy arose regarding the use of icons in worship—whether anyone other than God should create an image. The church in the East and West were divided on the issue. The Eastern Orthodox Church has continued to venerate icons, while the practice declined in the West in the Roman Catholic Church.

Iconography—both the *reading* and *writing* of icons—has made a comeback in the past century. The terms *reading* and *writing* refer to the belief that icons are not just religious art. We typically talk about art as something that is made—an expression of personal creativity. But icons are different. They are a liturgical form of worship. The word *liturgy* means a work of the people, and icons come from a rich history of a specific artistic interpretation. The *creation* of an icon is a form of prayer. Rather than the phrase *paint it*, the iconographer is said to *write it*. This involves training and significant practice. There are workshops available if you wish to learn this ancient tradition. Some of these trainings involve weekly meetings where participants gradually write an icon. Others involve time at retreat centers, with meetings every few months over the course of a year or two.

Part of the complexity of the process of *writing* an icon is the use of imagery. The icons are filled with imagery—the colors, the placement of the hands, the halos, flowers, birds—that communicates messages of the kingdom of God. For instance, red represents divinity and blue represents humanity, so Christ is often depicted as wearing both colors. Another example is that the hand or hands of Mary are always pointing at Jesus. The practice of praying with an icon opens one to the divine as one maintains a posture of meditation and acceptance of the message given *through* the icon.

An artist friend of mine has been studying the practice of writing icons for many years. She makes an annual retreat to an abbey in Idaho in order to learn from a master iconographer. In addition, she participates in a weekly lesson in the city in which she is located. Despite this dedicated commitment to the craft, she claims amateur status. The skill takes a lifetime to master, but the delight of the writing is present immediately. She is delighted when working with this sacred process. Recently, her training was moved online. This was a new experience for both the instructor and the students, and they wondered if it would be effective. After a couple of lessons in this format, my friend stated with delight that the process was not diminished. God could indeed work even through the Internet. A serendipity of the instruction was that the camera was pointed directly on the work of the iconographer. The students were able to watch the intricate work up close—something they could not do when meeting in person.

PRACTICE

For centuries, Christians have written and prayed with icons. And while it may feel uncomfortable or strange at first, I have experienced something of the mystery of Christ as I've worshiped with an icon. It is a rich tradition of symbolism and faith to explore, and there are many icons to choose from. Two of the most familiar are the *Christ Pantocrator*, mentioned previously, and the Old Testament Trinity. These and other icons are available online or in Catholic bookstores or retreat centers.

Praying Alone

- Select an icon with which you feel a connection. You often feel an immediate connection or are drawn to one based on your current life circumstances.
- Choose a quiet place with sufficient light to illuminate the icon—overhead or with candles placed in front of it.
- Simply gaze at the icon. Try not to control it; just allow your gaze to go where it is drawn.
- Notice your emotions and open yourself to hear what God may be communicating to you.
- Let the eyes of the person on the image penetrate your soul.

- Allow as much time as you need. Ten to fifteen minutes is a good span when beginning the practice.
- When sufficient time has passed, thank God and spend time journaling about any messages you received.

Leading a Group

When leading a group, avoid giving too much instruction. The goal is to have the participants experience the icon without being too analytical. After the initial experience of praying with the icon, offer instruction on the meaning of the symbols.

Cast the image on a screen or give each individual a print of an icon with which to pray. You might want to have a number of prints from which the participants can choose.

Give the following instructions:

- "We're going to spend time praying with an icon. It is an image of a religious figure." (Here you may choose to speak specifically about the icon that the group will be praying with.)
- "We'll lower the lights and spend a few moments settling in and offering this time to God."
- "When you're ready, gaze at the image. By this, I mean look at it in a 'soft' manner. Take in the entire image and then allow your eyes to go where they will. Don't try to control it."
- "Spend fifteen minutes with the icon. The chime will sound at the end of the time. You can stop then or remain with the icon as others leave."
- "Please leave in silence to respect those who wish to remain in prayer."

The next time the group is together, spend some time processing the experience of this prayer practice. There are often varying levels of experience with this prayer form.

❧

Concluding Thoughts

It is awe-inspiring to join with Christians who have been praying with these same images for centuries. I encourage you to visit an Eastern Orthodox church to see the beauty of the icons lining the walls and ceiling of the sanctuary. The priests are often available and pleased to tell you about the icons represented.

Additional Resources

Forest, Jim. *Praying with Icons*, rev. ed. Maryknoll, NY: Orbis Books, 2008.

Hales, Christine Simoneau. *Eyes of Fire: How Icons Saved My Life as an Artist*. n.l.: Christine Simoneau Hales, 2018.

Harrison, Nonna Verna. *God's Many Splendored Image: Theological Anthropology in Christian Formation*. Grand Rapids: Baker, 2010.

Mathewes-Green, Frederica. *The Open Door: Entering the Sanctuary of Icons and Prayer*. Brewster, MA: Paraclete Press, 2003.

Nouwen, Henri J. M. *Behold the Beauty of the Lord: Praying with Icons*. Notre Dame, IN: Ave Maria Press, 1987.

Note

[1]Justo L. Gonzalez, *The Story of Christianity*, vol. 2 (New York: HarperCollins, 2010), 157.

CHAPTER THIRTEEN

Process of Examen

The examen is a technique of prayerful reflection on the events of the day. It was my entrée into the rich treasure of the ancient church disciplines. I was introduced to the process when I was wrestling with a decision of whether I should go back to school for a PhD. I was torn on whether to continue my focus on growing a private practice as a marriage and family therapist (MFT) or get my advanced degree so that I could train other MFTs.

To help with my discernment, I was given the book *Sleeping with Bread: Holding What Gives You Life*, by Matthew Linn, Dennis Linn, and Sheila Fabricant Linn. It explained the discernment process of paying attention to what gives you life and what takes life from you. The idea is that the things that are life-giving for an individual reflect how God intended them to be. Simply put, you do more of what gives you life and less of what takes life from you.

As I began to pay attention to these inclinations, I realized that although I enjoy therapy, I felt the life drain out of me when I offered session after session. I needed variety and recovery time. This was in contrast to many of my MFT colleagues, who feel alive and invigorated after a session—the more sessions they do, the more alive they feel. On the other hand, there is nothing that gives me greater joy than teaching. It comes naturally to me! I revel in the process of preparation, the actual teaching, and getting to see the lightbulbs come on in my students.

This process of *listening* helped me discern that I wanted to choose teaching as my vocation. (The serendipity was that I would get to do both as a professor of MFT.) I began attending retreats offered by one of the authors of *Sleeping with Bread*. He was a Jesuit and became a trusted friend and mentor. My eyes were opened to the vast treasure of Christian disciplines that had been around for centuries. What a gift!

Background and History

The process of examen or examination of conscience was created by Ignatius of Loyola, whose background was introduced in Chapter Three. As mentioned previously, he had little to distract him during his convalescence except for the two books on the life of Christ and the lives of the saints. He spent days in thought vacillating between envisioning himself in the glories of battle and court and in a life of valor for the Lord and the church.

Over time, he became aware of a pattern in his heart that was related to his thoughts. When he thought of serving the Lord, he felt a rush of excitement and this passion was sustained. This feeling of exhilaration stayed with him. However, when he thought with passion of battle and the court, he recognized a similar initial rush of excitement but with a dry aftermath. He recognized in the process that God was calling him to serve the church. This is who he was made to be! He identified the first as consolation and the latter as desolation.

Later in his life when he founded the Jesuits, he shaped a practice of prayer around these two positions. He believed them to be ways that God communicates with us—they help us know who God made us to be. In its simplest form, we recognize through this awareness that God created us to do more of the things that give us life. Although nothing is free of challenge, when we are aware of desolation in our lives, we do less of it or address it in some way—particularly by inviting God into the situation. Both help us center our lives on God.

One caveat is that it is often the case that we go through times when desolation is a constant companion. We may plead with God to remove a situation, but God does not honor our request. It is in these times that we cling to God and trust in his faithfulness. An example might be helpful for further exploring this concept. I was once in an abusive employment position that lasted for a number of years. I pleaded with God to remove me from this situation but to no avail. I despaired, as I couldn't understand what God was doing. How was I to live fully and become who God made me to be when I was being mistreated?

It was in hindsight that I recognized the consolation in this situation. I loved my job and colleagues, despite the abuse dished out by one particular individual. I drew close to God during this time. That was the most significant consolation of all! It was a long, difficult road, but I now recognize that I gained so much. I came to realize my utter dependence on God through this struggle. And it was during this time that I learned about contemplative prayer and became trained as a spiritual director. My ministry in spiritual formation came to life. I wonder if this would have occurred had I been free of this abusive situation. I was forced to my knees and learned to find consolation despite the abuse. Although it was a dark time, I was richly blessed. I cannot adequately express my gratitude for developing a relationship with God on this deeper level. I would not wish this experience on anyone, but I can truly say I would go through it again for this end. What I learned in this situation was to trust in God's faithful presence. I was never alone. God gave me consolation in the midst of desolation.

Thus the benefit of examen is that it helps me "pray without ceasing" (1 Thess. 5:17 NASB). With time, it assists us in developing a lens through which we see God at the center of our daily activities. Through examen, I become increasingly mindful of God's presence and the opportunities I have to serve as an instrument of the kingdom. It creates a continual awareness of the presence of God.

PRACTICE

Praying Alone

It is intended that the practice be short, requiring no more than fifteen minutes. It is generally practiced twice a day—with the first instance in the morning and the second at noon or in the evening. The point is to review the previous day and then have a second time to reinforce that mindset.

There are a number of formats for the prayer:

- The simple format of two questions, as articulated by the Linns:[1]
  - Ask yourself one of the following sets of questions:
    - What brings me life?
    - What takes life from me?
      OR
    - For what am I most grateful?
    - For what am I least grateful?
      OR

- ◆ When have I felt the most loved?
- ◆ When have I felt the least loved?
  - ▪ Record your responses in a journal. Keep your answers short.
  - ▪ Look back periodically and observe the emerging patterns. These patterns can assist in discernment.

- Another format taught by Mark Thibodeaux in his book *Reimagining the Ignatian Examen:*[2]
  - ▪ Give thanks for the day.
  - ▪ Ask for the Spirit to open your eyes to what you need to acknowledge.
  - ▪ Review and recognize failures.
  - ▪ Ask for forgiveness and healing.
  - ▪ Pray about the next day.

- The original structure as taught by Ignatius:
  - ▪ General examen
    - ◆ Prayer for enlightenment—That the Spirit will help me see myself a bit more as he sees me.
    - ◆ Reflective thanksgiving—Rest in genuine faith-filled gratitude to our Father for his gifts in this most recent part of the day.
    - ◆ Practical survey of actions—What has been happening in and through me since my last examen?
  - ▪ Particular examen
    - ◆ Repeat the previously noted format in regard to how you can be led by the Spirit in a *specific* situation.
  - ▪ Contrition and sorrow
    - ◆ Recall the ways in which you have walked outside of God's will.

- Note: This contrition and sorrow is not shame or depression at our weakness but a faith experience as we grow in our realization of our Father's awesome desire that we love him with every ounce of our being.
- Hopeful resolution for the future
  - Gratitude and a celebration in our relationship with God.
  - Note: A great hope, founded in our Father whose victory in Jesus Christ we share through the life of the Spirit in our hearts, should be the atmosphere of our hearts at this point.

Leading a Group

Large groups

When leading a group in this prayer, break the group into smaller groups of three to four people. This allows for vulnerability and will take around fifteen to twenty minutes. Encourage them to keep their sharing somewhat brief, in order to allow equal opportunity for all. It is helpful to write the questions on a whiteboard.

- Give the following instructions:
  - "Each person in the group will answer the following questions:
    - What brings me life?
    - What takes life from me?"
  - "It is important to share both that which is life-giving and life-taking, as they are both vital to the process."
  - "After everyone has answered the two questions, go around the circle again and take turns praying for the person on your right. Focus your prayer on the consolations and desolations shared by the individual."

I use this practice on all the retreats I lead. Without exception, the group develops a trust and intimacy as they share at this level of depth—especially as they articulate their struggles.

A side note in regard to sharing struggles: It is often the case that some try to avoid sharing the desolation (what is life-taking). There are a number of reasons for this. First, it comes from the mindset that Christians *should* be happy and free of pain. If we are faithful, God will bless us—a form of the prosperity gospel. Or it might come from a fear of vulnerability. Rationales come in some form of "I try not to dwell on the negative" or "I just keep my eyes fixed on Jesus and don't worry about the bad." Although these sound "right," they can quickly hinder a group from growing closer.

Small ongoing groups

- Designate a recorder to note the responses of each participant.
- Have each person answer the two questions.
- Pray for the person on your right.
- Periodically (at the end of your time together or at a designated time, such as six months later), go back and review the recorded responses.
- Discuss any themes that have arisen for each person.

Families

- Share consolations and desolations at the dinner table. Use more simplistic words such as "best" and "worst."
- Praise God for your blessings and invite God into your struggles.

Concluding Thoughts

As a family, we began this practice when our daughters were three and seven years old. We did it at dinner each night by sharing our "best" and "worst" for the day. (Our three-year-old typically used it as an opportunity to tattle on her big sister.) It was sweet to hear the concerns and joys of the girls. Sometimes we were surprised as we learned about difficult things that they had not yet shared with us. As parents, this gave us the opportunity to share our concerns and set a good example for our daughters as they developed their relationship with God. We kept up with this practice for many years until our daughters became teenagers. Crazy activity schedules and sports cut our time together at night significantly. It then evolved into a practice that occurred on special occasions.

Additional Resources

Gallagher, Timothy M. *The Examen Prayer: Ignatian Wisdom for Our Lives Today.* New York: Crosswords, 2006.

Ignatius of Loyola. *The Spiritual Exercises of St. Ignatius: Or Manresa.* New York: TAN Books, 1999.

Linn, Dennis, Sheila Fabricant-Linn, and Matthew Linn. *Sleeping with Bread: Holding What Gives You Life,* 1st ed. Mahwah, NJ: Paulist Press, 1995.

Thibodeaux, Mark E. *Reimagining the Ignatian Examen: Fresh Ways to Pray from Your Day.* Chicago: Loyola Press, 2015.

Notes

[1] Dennis Linn, Sheila Fabricant Linn, and Matthew Linn, *Sleeping with Bread: Holding What Gives You Life,* 1st ed. (Mahwah: Paulist Press, 1995).

[2] Mark E. Thibodeaux, *Reimagining the Ignatian Examen: Fresh Ways to Pray from Your Day.* (Chicago: Loyola Press, 2015), 103–10.

CHAPTER FOURTEEN

Centering Prayer

Centering prayer is a practice that emphasizes emptying one's mind in order to open oneself fully for God's shaping. When I began my journey with contemplative prayer, I had a difficult time finding a community who understood and were practitioners of the prayer forms. The discovery of the program on Contemplative Prayer Leaders at the Shalem Institute for Spiritual Formation was like coming home for me. Here was a group that put words to the life experience I had with God. In them, I found an understanding that God loves us and is eager to have an intimate relationship with all of creation.

My training in contemplative prayer was rich. I relished every moment. However, my reentry into normal life was rough. It was a familiar coming-off-the-mountain experience, and with it came a longing for the depth of community well-versed in contemplative prayer. Although I was in the Bible Belt, few knew about these prayer forms. I searched for a while and eventually found a centering prayer group in our community. This group utilized a particular form of contemplative prayer.

The group of eight welcomed me into their circle, pleased to teach me about the prayer form. We met once a week and began our time by watching a short video of Fr. Thomas Keating, one of the creators of the prayer.[1] We then had a thirty-minute "sit"—a time of doing centering prayer together in silence. I grew to love this small group of friends and the practice of centering prayer. I prayed and shared life with this group for a number of years until I moved to another state.

The practice had taken hold, and it was not long before I located a group in my new locale. The content of the meetings of the new group varied slightly from that of the previous group, but had at its heart the practice of centering prayer. We typically check in with each other and take turns bringing a reading that has had an impact on our life and faith. Then we do a thirty-minute sit. These people are very dear to me, and although I rarely see them outside of our prayer time, I consider them some of my closest friends. It's almost mystical; although half of our time spent in these group sessions is in silence, the sense of the Spirit and the common heart is palpable.

Our group was unable to meet in person for a time, so we decided to meet by Zoom. This offered a lovely alternative. Although we were eager to be in each other's physical presence, our prayer together over Zoom was sweet. We were able to follow our same routine of check-in, reading, and prayer in the virtual platform.

Background and History

Thomas Keating was the abbot of a Trappist abbey, St. Joseph's, in Massachusetts in the sixties and seventies. There were many retreat centers in the vicinity—Christian and others. He noticed that many young people who had grown up in the church would travel to the retreat centers of the Eastern faith traditions seeking depth and meaning. These travelers would often stop for the night at St. Joseph's. Fr. Keating, along with Basil Pennington and William Meninger, two of the monks at the abbey, decided to create a contemplative prayer form that was accessible to these travelers but had Christ at its heart. They called it *centering prayer*, based on a description of contemplative prayer by Thomas Merton—"prayer that is centered entirely on the presence of God."[2]

The prayer form caught on, and the three men began offering workshops and retreats. From this small beginning, the Contemplative Outreach movement was formed. There is now a worldwide network of people who practice centering prayer. Groups and training are available in most cities, and many locales have annual conferences that include speakers, training, and the opportunity to network with other centering prayer practitioners.

PRACTICE

Contemplative Outreach lays out the following steps for centering prayer:

1. Choose a sacred word as a symbol of your intention to consent to God's presence and action within.
2. Sitting comfortably and with eyes closed, settle briefly and silently introduce the sacred word as the symbol of your consent to God's presence and action within.
3. When engaged with your thoughts (including body sensations, feelings, images, and reflections), return ever so gently to the sacred word.
4. At the end of the prayer period, remain in silence with eyes closed for a couple of minutes.

The typical time for a "sit" is twenty to thirty minutes, twice a day. It is encouraged that along with private daily sits, each individual find a group with which to pray.

Concluding Thoughts

The most challenging aspect of centering prayer is dealing with the thoughts that intrude while in prayer. Author Cynthia Bourgeault tells a story of a nun who struggled with this. In one of the very earliest training workshops, led by Thomas Keating, the nun tried out her first twenty-minute taste of centering prayer and then lamented, "Oh, Father Thomas, I'm such a failure at this prayer. In twenty minutes, I've had ten thousand thoughts." "How lovely," responded Keating, without missing a beat. "Ten thousand opportunities to return to God!"[3]

The nun's experience is common. Initially, it is difficult to let go of one's thoughts. Like all worthwhile endeavors, it takes practice to learn to avoid engaging in the myriad of thoughts that press in. The following recommendation has been helpful when thoughts emerge during my prayers: Rather than trying to force yourself not to think (like trying to make yourself go to sleep), gently place the intruding thoughts on a boat and let them float down the river. Don't get into the boat; just watch it go past from your position on the shore. When you realize you are in the boat or even steering the boat, gently slip back into the water and let the boat go on. It's important not to fight the thoughts but notice them and let them go.

Additional Resources

Bourgeault, Cynthia. *Centering Prayer and Inner Awakening*. Lanham, MD: Cowley Publications, 2004.

Keating, Thomas. *Open Mind, Open Heart: The Contemplative Dimension of the Gospel.* New York: Continuum, 1995.

Pennington, M. Basil. *Centering Prayer: Renewing an Ancient Prayer Form.* New York: Doubleday, 1982.

Notes

[1] For more on Thomas Keating and centering prayer, see Thomas Keating, *Open Mind, Open Heart: The Contemplative Dimension of the Gospel* (New York: Continuum, 1995).

[2] Thomas Merton, *Contemplative Prayer* (New York: Random House, 1969), 6.

[3] Cynthia Bourgeault, *Centering Prayer and Inner Awakening* (Lanham, MD: Cowley Publications, 2004), 23.

CHAPTER FIFTEEN

The Jesus Prayer

The Jesus Prayer is a short meditative "breath prayer." It is said repeatedly with the intent of centering ourselves on Jesus.

For a number of years, I taught a course at the undergraduate level called "Disciplines for Christian Living." It was considered a Bible course and fulfilled a semester requirement. There were two versions: one for Bible majors—those preparing for a role in ministry—and the other for everyone else. I preferred teaching those who were not pursuing a vocation with the church. I appreciated their fresh perspective and the opportunity to introduce these students to the disciplines.

The class experienced the disciplines in two ways: First, each week throughout the fifteen-week semester, students would practice a different discipline. Second, from the list of disciplines, they chose two to three to practice for the entire semester. The disciplines varied from fasting to service to prayer forms. Almost without exception, one of the favorites of the class was the Jesus Prayer. The students quickly realized that it could be used with ease in any context. Many spoke of the manner in which it helped with anxiety in the moment or gave them a way to center on Jesus throughout the day. One student athlete became a zealous evangelist for the prayer form. He began the course slumped in his chair, frustrated that he had to waste his time with these religious classes. But, after practicing it for one week, he realized its value. He used the prayer before and during games when he needed to still his mind and center himself, and he encouraged many of his fellow athletes to use it.

Background and History

The Jesus Prayer, "Lord Jesus Christ, Son of God, have mercy on me, a sinner," is based on various pleas made to Jesus in the Gospels. Matthew 9:27, Mark 10:47, and Luke 18:38 record this plea coming from blind men. The Canaanite woman in Matthew 15:22 and lepers in Luke 17:13 also voiced this plea. It became a popular prayer in the early church and is considered the most famous of the monastic prayers. It is also one of the main spiritual practices of the Eastern Church. The first recorded use of this plea in repetition was in the sixth century. Monks were encouraged to repeat the phrase with the purpose of following the encouragement by Paul to "pray without ceasing" (1 Thess. 5:17 NASB). It assisted monks in attaining inner silence and deepening their relationship with Jesus.

The practice became popular in the West through a tale of an anonymous pilgrim, *The Way of the Pilgrim*. It tells of a spiritual seeker in nineteenth-century Russia who sought the advice of a spiritual father on how to live out the apostle Paul's mandate of unceasing prayer. The elder taught the pilgrim the Jesus Prayer and encouraged him to say it repeatedly—until the prayer became as familiar and unconscious as his own breath. He told him to fight distractions and "be patient and peaceful and repeat the process frequently."[1] Gregory of Sinai said that this practice was meant to help individuals still the mind and concentrate "on the approaching presence of the merciful Christ, a presence that is announced by a definite 'warming of the heart.'"[2]

This is a prayer form that I return to on occasion. I have practiced it throughout the day in imitation of the Russian pilgrim, although I did not get up to ten thousand prayers, as he did. It does center all of one's thoughts on Christ as you say his name repeatedly through the hours. In addition, I often share this prayer form with individuals who come to me for spiritual direction. It is a helpful practice in times of stress or anxiety—the words are a comfort and the concentrated focus on the breath helps slow down the rate of breathing.

PRACTICE

Praying Alone

The practice of the Jesus Prayer is quite simple. It can be done in a formal or informal manner. If practicing formally, find a quiet place that is comfortable and free of distraction.

- Gregory of Sinai suggested that the posture of the body can assist in the intent of the prayer. He recommended that the pray-er sit on a low stool in order to "drag down the intellect into the heart."[3]
- As you begin, slow down your breathing and allow it to match the phrases of the prayer. While breathing out, say, "Lord Jesus Christ, Son of God," and while breathing in, say, "Have mercy on me, a sinner." This can be said out loud or silently.

- Repeat this prayer until you are able to let go of your thoughts and be fully centered on Christ. It can be helpful to set a timer, so you aren't distracted by watching the time.
- Some other phrases are used as well:
  - "Lord Jesus, have mercy on me"
  - "Lord Jesus, have mercy"
  - "Jesus"

When practicing informally, pray the Jesus Prayer as you go about your daily activities. Use the same format, saying the prayer on the exhale and inhale. Some suggestions include:

- Set a timer to chime on the hour, reminding you to pray.
- State the prayer at the beginning and end of the day and whenever it comes to mind.
- Wear a bracelet or rubber band around your wrist. Use it as a reminder to pray each time you notice it.

Leading a Group

You can either have the group repeat the prayer together or send them out to pray on their own. If you are praying together, use the following instructions:

- "Get in a comfortable position and take everything off your lap. Hold your hands in an open posture."
- "As you begin, slow down your breathing and allow it to match the phrases of the prayer. On the exhale, say, 'Lord Jesus Christ, Son of God,' and on the inhale, say, 'have mercy on me, a sinner.' I will lead us in saying it together."
- "We will repeat the prayer for a few minutes to allow us to let go of our thoughts and be fully centered on Christ. I'll sound a chime as we begin our last time saying it."

- "After we are finished, we'll spend a few moments in silence and then have a time of sharing."
- "Let's begin. (In a slow and meditative manner) Jesus Christ, Son of God (Pause), have mercy on me, a sinner." Repeat for about five minutes.

Sound the chime as you begin your last exhale to signal that you are about to stop. Allow a few moments of silence and then have participants share their experience with the person next to them. Sound the chime and call the attention of the group. Ask if there are a few who would like to share with the whole group. This draws the group together and elicits a sense of shared experience. If sending them out on their own, give them the following instructions:

- "We're going to practice the Jesus Prayer alone. Find a place to sit inside or outside, or walk while you pray."
- "We'll come back together in fifteen minutes. Set a timer so you don't have to check the time."
- "As you begin, slow down your breathing and allow it to match the phrases of the prayer. On the exhale, say, 'Lord Jesus Christ, Son of God,' and on the inhale, say, 'have mercy on me, a sinner.'"
- "At the end of the fifteen minutes, come back to the room, and we'll process our experiences together."

When participants return, ask them to share their experiences with the person next to them. Then call the attention of the group and ask if there are a few who would like to share with the entire group.

Concluding Thoughts

As my students discovered while practicing the Jesus Prayer, this prayer form is one of the few practices that can be used immediately, in any context. In its informal use, there is no need to create space or sit and close your eyes. Many use it upon waking when they can't go back to sleep. Others have reported using it while they wait to see their dentist or doctor or any time they feel anxious. Still others practice it with the intent of the Russian pilgrim, to keep their hearts and minds centered on God as they go about their day. It can truly help us pray without ceasing.

Additional Resources

Bacovcin, Helen, trans. *The Way of a Pilgrim and the Pilgrim Continues His Way*. New York: Image Books, 1978.

Mathewes-Green, Frederica. *The Jesus Prayer: The Ancient Desert Prayer That Tunes the Heart to God*. Brewster, MA: Paraclete Press, 2009.

———. *Praying the Jesus Prayer*. Brewster, MA: Paraclete Press, 2011.

Notes

[1] Helen Bacovcin, trans., *The Way of a Pilgrim and the Pilgrim Continues His Way* (New York: Image Books, 1978), 10.

[2] Gordon Mursell, *The Story of Christian Spirituality: Two Thousand Years from East to West* (Minneapolis: Fortress Press, 2001), 148.

[3] Mursell, *The Story of Christian Spirituality*, 148.

CHAPTER SIXTEEN

Stations of the Cross

The Stations of the Cross are a mini-pilgrimage of the *Via Dolorosa* (the Way of Suffering) or Way of the Cross (*Via Crucis*)—a devotion involving the sites and experiences of the day of Christ's death. The stations are fourteen depictions chronicling this day, beginning with his condemnation and ending with his being laid in the tomb. These numbered stations are arranged at regular intervals in many church sanctuaries and along paths located close to churches. They are also found at most retreat centers. Participants stop before each Station, taking time to say accompanying prayers and meditate on the scene depicted. They then move on to the next.

The images are sculptures, raised reliefs, paintings, or carvings made out of stone, wood, or metal. There are variations, but the standard set is as follows:

1. Jesus is condemned to death by Pilate.
2. Jesus is made to bear his cross.

3. Jesus falls the first time.
4. Jesus meets his mother.
5. Simon of Cyrene is made to bear the cross.
6. Veronica wipes Jesus's face.
7. Jesus falls the second time.
8. The women of Jerusalem weep over Jesus.
9. Jesus falls the third time.
10. Jesus is stripped of his garments.
11. Jesus is nailed to the cross.
12. Jesus dies on the cross.
13. Jesus is taken down from the cross.
14. Jesus is placed in the tomb.

I have prayed with these beautiful works of art in many locations around the country. As with all of these contemplative prayer forms, God meets me where I am in the moment, regardless of how often I pray. Each occasion offers a unique experience.

Background and History

One of the first known accounts of the history of the Stations of the Cross was written in the early twentieth century. In his account, Herbert Thurston writes of the legend of Mary, the mother of Jesus, setting stones down along the path to commemorate the passion of her son. It is said she walked this path daily.[1] Other followers of Jesus imitated the practice as they sought to follow in his footsteps, retracing his steps from the house of Pilate to the tomb. Although the origin of the devotion is not known, it was the Franciscans who popularized the practice during the time of the crusades.

St. Francis had a particular affinity for Christ's passion, and thus it is logical that he would have been devoted to this practice. Raised in a wealthy family, he forsook his privilege and embraced suffering and poverty in imitation of Christ. During the crusades,

Francis and his followers were given a special allowance to the Holy Lands to guard and promote devotion to certain holy sites. This was due to a relationship developed with the Sultan of Egypt. Francis went to Egypt to convert the sultan and spent three days with him. The sultan did not convert, but tradition holds that he said, "I would convert to your religion as it is a beautiful one, but we would both be murdered." The Franciscans were the only order to receive permission to care for these holy sites—one being the *Via Dolorosa.*

Promotion of the Way of Suffering eventually led the Franciscans to offer the opportunity outside of the Holy Land. Believers wanted to experience this devotion in their own lands, as many did not have the means to travel to the Holy Land. The Franciscans were granted permission to create replicas of the *Via Dolorosa* in churches across Europe, which led to the creation of the Stations of the Cross.[2]

Praying the Stations of the Cross has been a popular ritual through the centuries—particularly during Lent, with a focus on Good Friday. Praying the stations during Lent provides the opportunity for increased devotion to the suffering of Christ. It deepens the pascal experience as one meditates on the events of that day. It is also beneficial, however, to observe the devotion on any given day throughout the year. It is my practice to walk through the stations once or twice during a retreat, a common practice for retreatants. I often include the experience as a group prayer in the retreats I lead.

My initial impetus for practicing this prayer form was curiosity. I saw these numbered images in churches and on retreat grounds and wanted to look more closely at the art and discover their meaning. At some point, I discovered the devotions that accompanied the stations, along with the deeper meaning attributed to each. These are easy to find, as there are many sources online and in print that offer meditations and scripture on the theme of each station. They typically are comprised of an opening prayer, a scripture, a meditation about what Jesus is experiencing at each station, and a closing prayer—sometimes the Lord's Prayer or Gloria.

The more I have prayed with the Stations of the Cross, the more I have been blessed by this rich practice. The gifts received have evolved over the years. There is nothing sweeter than slowing down the events of that day in the life of Jesus and meditating on them. The more I learn about my Lord, the more deeply I love him. But beyond learning *about* the passion of Christ is when I lay my life and struggle alongside that of my Lord. That is the deeper meaning of this devotion. I learned this over time, but there is one instance that was particularly poignant. I was on a silent retreat during a time in my life when I was struggling. The spiritual director encouraged me to pray with the stations, bringing my pain to Jesus and seeking an understanding of his experience. As I went from station to station, the eyes of my heart were opened to the way the experience of Christ spoke to my pain. Each station addressed a different aspect of the pain of Christ in relation to the pain of the world. I was reminded at a deeper level that Christ, my high priest, understands all that I have lived through. This was a great grace to be given, and I have carried it with me for years.

As I continued the practice, however, I was given an even deeper gift. I had been wrestling for years with some difficult experiences from which I was not being released. I had asked to be free of them, but that did not seem to be how God was answering my prayers. This request continued across many silent retreats, and I began to realize that God was inviting me to a deeper way of being in relation to my suffering. It was about finding joy in my suffering. The invitation was not the idea of finding joy *despite* my suffering (finding the silver lining) but of finding joy *within* my suffering—experiencing it as a means to enter into the suffering of my Lord. This was a new concept for me but so evident in Scripture: "Count it all joy, my brothers, when you meet trials of various kinds, for you know that the testing of your faith produces steadfastness. And let steadfastness have its full effect, that you may be perfect and complete, lacking in nothing" (James 1:2–4 ESV). "More than that, we rejoice in our sufferings, knowing that suffering produces endurance, and endurance produces character, and character produces hope, and hope does not disappoint us, because God's love has been poured into our hearts through the Holy Spirit which has been given to us" (Rom. 5:3–5 RSV).

I lacked this means of understanding suffering due to the entitled Western culture in which I had been raised and lived my life. But God would not let me ignore it. The Spirit kept bringing me back to this concept year after year when I came on retreat. I so wanted to understand but was not able to align my heart with my desire to be grateful for suffering. But finally, God in his mercy got through to me. As I began another eight-day silent retreat, I went into the church sanctuary to pray with the stations. I was going to journal at each station—again, laying the suffering of Christ alongside my own suffering. As had been my previous experience, I knew that I would receive comfort as I saw how Christ understands what I was going through because of his suffering. Thus, I proceeded in this way for the first four stations and then fell short. I sensed the Spirit's invitation to take myself out of the center and put Christ there. I realized in that moment that it really was not about me. The suffering I endured was allowing me in some small way to experience what Christ had endured. It allowed me to enter into his suffering, to understand his gift more deeply.

The grace of this depth in no way lessened by my previous experience with the Stations of the Cross. I continue to learn more about Christ's passion and to be blessed with peace, knowing that he does understand! It has made my experience broader and richer.

Praying Alone

It is important to give yourself sufficient time to pray the stations. You can spend a half hour with the prayer, devoting a minute or two to each if you read quickly through the meditations. This is a good way to introduce yourself to the practice. A longer length of time, however, gives you the opportunity to stop at a station when you are given a prompt from the Spirit that you may need to spend additional time in prayer with that theme. Having a journal with you allows you to capture any insights given as you pray.

- Whether outside or in a church sanctuary, find the first station and, before beginning, pause and take a few deep breaths. Breathe in God's love and light and breathe out any concerns or worries you are carrying. Be fully present to what you are about to experience.
- Offer yourself to God and ask for guidance as you pray.
- At each station, gaze at the image.
  - Allow your eyes to fall where they will and just let yourself absorb what you are seeing.
  - Read the meditation slowly, looking at the image from time to time.
  - If desired, spend time journaling. Just write down whatever comes to you; don't try to control it.
  - When you finish the meditation, gaze for a while longer at the image before moving to the next station.
- After you finish the final station:
  - Offer a prayer of thanksgiving.

▪ Spend time journaling about the entire devotion.

Leading a Group

When leading a retreat, I bring booklets or handouts for each participant. Praying the stations together is a rich time of communion for a group. The experience is in silence, apart from the reading of the meditations.

- Gather the group near the first station. Assign the reading parts. I will often have the participants take turns being the "leader" for each station. If there are fewer than fourteen people, they will serve as the leader for more than one station each. It can be helpful to give them paper numbers to assist in remembering the ones to which they are assigned.
- Then give the following instructions:
    ▪ "We'll begin with the first station. I will read the opening prayer."
    ▪ "The leader will say all parts assigned to the leader along with the scripture and meditation. The followers will read the parts assigned to 'all' in unison."
    ▪ "When finished with a station, walk to the next in a slow, meditative way."
    ▪ "Keep track of when it is your turn to serve as the leader."
    ▪ "When we are finished, leave in silence."

Pause for a few moments of silence after the final "Amen" of a station meditation and then head to the next. If meeting immediately after the experience, have a time of debriefing. This allows for a deepening of the prayer. I encourage those in the group to find time to pray the stations on their own—especially if it is a new experience to them.

Opening Prayer

The following is a meditation for each station:

Dear God, open our hearts to what you have for us in this holy journey to the cross. Heighten our understanding of Christ's love made visible through each station. Help us commit anew to living this love with each person we encounter—seeing them with eyes enhanced through your suffering. Amen.

Station 1—Jesus is condemned to death

Leader: We adore you, O Christ, and we praise you.

All: Because by your cross you have redeemed the world.

> Pilate said to them, "Then what shall I do with Jesus who is called Christ?" They all said, "Let him be crucified!" And he said, "Why? What evil has he done?" But they shouted all the more, "Let him be crucified!" So when Pilate saw that he was gaining nothing, but rather that a riot was beginning, he took water and washed his hands before the crowd, saying, "I am innocent of this man's blood; see to it yourselves." And all the people answered, "His blood be on us and on our children!" Then he released for them Barabbas, and having scourged Jesus, delivered him to be crucified. (Matt. 27:22–26 ESV)

Jesus, you stand alone before Pilate. How difficult to hear the mocking crowd, the jeering soldiers, and a sentence of death. Everything you did was for the salvation of these people, yet they have turned on you. Even those closest to you have fled, leaving you to your fate.

I too have felt abandoned at times, Lord. I have been criticized unjustly and treated unfairly. I am afraid at times and feel I have nowhere to turn. Yet I am not alone. You are with me and understand my pain.

Leader: Jesus Christ, Son of God

All: Have mercy on us.

All: Glory be to the Father, and to the Son, and to the Holy Spirit, as it was in the beginning, is now, and ever shall be, world without end. Amen.

Station 2—Jesus is made to bear his cross

Leader: We adore you, O Christ, and we praise you.

All: Because by your cross you have redeemed the world.

> Then the soldiers of the governor took Jesus into the governor's headquarters, and they gathered the whole battalion before him. And they stripped him and put a scarlet robe on him, and twisting together a crown of thorns, they put it on his head and put a reed in his right hand. And kneeling before him, they mocked him, saying, "Hail, King of the Jews!" And they spit on him and took the reed and struck him on the head. And when they had mocked him, they stripped him of the robe and put his own clothes on him and led him away to crucify him. (Matt. 27:27–31 ESV)

Lord, the cross they placed on you was a heavy cross. You were in no shape to bear it. It was rough and coarse and was not placed on you with any sort of kindness. I know you were fully aware of this abuse and that you were carrying the cross to your death. Yet you accepted the cross. You took this heavy burden without complaint.

There are burdens that I must bear at times, Lord. They are heavy—sometimes so heavy, I think I will be crushed. Give me the courage and the strength to bear these burdens with the grace I see in you.

Leader: Jesus Christ, Son of God
All: Have mercy on us.
All: Glory be to the Father, and to the Son, and to the Holy Spirit, as it was in the beginning, is now, and ever shall be, world without end. Amen.

Station 3—Jesus falls the first time

Leader: We adore you, O Christ, and we praise you.
All: Because by your cross you have redeemed the world.

> Come to me, all who labor and are heavy laden, and I will give you rest. Take my yoke upon you and learn from me, for I am gentle and lowly in heart, and you will find rest for your souls. For my yoke is easy and my burden is light. (Matt. 11:28–30 ESV)

Jesus, you fall under the weight of the cross. You are beaten and bruised, weary both in body and soul. Those around you continue to heap on the abuse. They are not interested in helping you. Yet you persevere. You continue on the path to the cross.

I know the burden you bear is for me, Lord. And, I know you continue to carry me even now. I get discouraged and want to give up. The weight of my load seems too heavy. At times, I do give up and neglect to do the things that I need to do. Give me the courage to persevere as you did.

Leader: Jesus Christ, Son of God
All: Have mercy on us.
All: Glory be to the Father, and to the Son, and to the Holy Spirit, as it was in the beginning, is now, and ever shall be, world without end. Amen.

Station 4—Jesus meets his mother

Leader: We adore you, O Christ, and we praise you.

All: Because by your cross you have redeemed the world.

> And let us consider how to stir up one another to love
> and good works, not neglecting to meet together, as
> is the habit of some, but encouraging one another,
> and all the more as you see the Day drawing near.
> (Heb. 10:24–25 ESV)

In the midst of the pain and confusion, you see a familiar face, Lord. You see the face of your mother. She cannot take away your pain, but she is with you in your suffering. And for that moment, your struggle lessens.

Thank you for community, Lord. Thank you for those you place in our lives who walk alongside us in our pain. And thank you for the opportunities you present for us to walk alongside others in their suffering.

Leader: Jesus Christ, Son of God
All: Have mercy on us.
All: Glory be to the Father, and to the Son, and to the Holy Spirit, as it was in the beginning, is now, and ever shall be, world without end. Amen.

Station 5—Simon of Cyrene is made to bear the cross
Leader: We adore you, O Christ, and we praise you.
All: Because by your cross you have redeemed the world.

> As they went out, they found a man of Cyrene, Simon
> by name. They compelled this man to carry his cross.
> (Matt. 27:32 ESV)

Jesus, you are faltering, and the guards grab someone from the crowd to help you. Simon may have been a curious bystander, or he may have been heaping insults on you. Regardless, out of no choice of his own, he became your helper. You accept his help and continue on your journey.

There are times when I resist helping, Lord. There is need all around me, yet I find it easier to stay busy and forget that I am serving you when I help others. "Truly, I say to you, as you did it to one of the least of these my brothers, you did it to me" (Matt. 25:40 ESV). Open my eyes to see how I can best serve as your instrument.

Leader: Jesus Christ, Son of God

All: Have mercy on us.

All: Glory be to the Father, and to the Son, and to the Holy Spirit, as it was in the beginning, is now, and ever shall be, world without end. Amen.

Station 6—Veronica wipes Jesus's face

Leader: We adore you, O Christ, and we praise you.

All: Because by your cross you have redeemed the world.

> Do not neglect to do good and to share what you have,
> for such sacrifices are pleasing to God. (Heb. 13:16 ESV)

According to Christian tradition, a woman named Veronica came out of the crowd and wiped Jesus's face with a cloth. As a gift to her for her kindness, Jesus gave her an image of his face on the cloth. This small act of kindness was not typical of the angry crowd sending Jesus to the cross. It took courage for her to stand against the crowd.

There are times, Lord, when I also see opportunities to do good that may go against the wishes of the crowd. It may be the need to befriend a marginalized person or speak up against injustice. Give me eyes to see and the courage to do what is right.

Leader: Jesus Christ, Son of God

All: Have mercy on us.

All: Glory be to the Father, and to the Son, and to the Holy Spirit, as it was in the beginning, is now, and ever shall be, world without end. Amen.

Station 7—Jesus falls the second time
Leader: We adore you, O Christ, and we praise you.
All: Because by your cross you have redeemed the world.

> Rejoice always, pray without ceasing, give thanks in all circumstances; for this is the will of God in Christ Jesus for you. (1 Thess. 5:16–18 ESV)

Jesus, you are both divine and human. We see you in all your humanity as you stumble and fall a second time. The cross is becoming heavier and more difficult to bear. You do not give up; you fight your way up and persevere.

It is easy, Lord, to feel sorry for myself when I am struggling. Sometimes, I can accept a struggle as the cross I need to bear. However, if it goes on too long, I begin to feel neglected—like you have forgotten me. Keep my eyes on you, Jesus. Give me a heart of gratitude and peace, so when the burden is heavy, I will gladly shoulder it in service to you.

Leader: Jesus Christ, Son of God
All: Have mercy on us.
All: Glory be to the Father, and to the Son, and to the Holy Spirit, as it was in the beginning, is now, and ever shall be, world without end. Amen.

Station 8—The women of Jerusalem weep over Jesus
Leader: We adore you, O Christ, and we praise you.
All: Because by your cross you have redeemed the world.

> A large number of people followed him, including
> women who mourned and wailed for him. Jesus turned
> and said to them, "Daughters of Jerusalem, do not
> weep for me; weep for yourselves and for your children."
> (Luke 23:27–28)

Jesus, as you continue on your way, you encounter a group of women who are distressed at your suffering. Without thinking of yourself and in the midst of your pain, you stop and offer comfort to them. Even as you are abandoned and without encouragement, you are able to rise above yourself and look to the needs of others.

Give us, your church, this desire and ability, Lord, to keep our eyes on the needs of the world. And give me this desire and ability. I can be so egocentric. As you did so throughout your life and particularly on this difficult journey, help me seek to bless others who are in pain.

Leader: Jesus Christ, Son of God
All: Have mercy on us.
All: Glory be to the Father, and to the Son, and to the Holy Spirit, as it was in the beginning, is now, and ever shall be, world without end. Amen.

Station 9—Jesus falls the third time
Leader: We adore you, O Christ, and we praise you.
All: Because by your cross you have redeemed the world.

> Again, for the second time, he went away and prayed,
> "My Father, if this cannot pass unless I drink it, your will
> be done." And again, he came and found them sleep-
> ing, for their eyes were heavy. So, leaving them again,
> he went away and prayed for the third time, saying the
> same words again. (Matt. 26:42–44 ESV)

Jesus, you fall yet again, a third time. You are weary, and it is so challenging to keep going. You ask God repeatedly for release from this suffering, but God does not take it away. So, you persevere—you struggle up and put one foot in front of the other, continuing faithfully on the way God has set before you. You continue on the path to the cross.

Lord, sometimes I grow weary from the struggles of life—especially when it seems too heavy to bear. I find myself questioning your faithfulness as the pain is not removed. In this third fall, you show me that you understand the weariness of continuing suffering. You are with me in my pain. Again, Lord, keep the eyes of my heart on you.

Leader: Jesus Christ, Son of God
All: Have mercy on us.
All: Glory be to the Father, and to the Son, and to the Holy Spirit, as it was in the beginning, is now, and ever shall be, world without end. Amen.

Station 10—Jesus is stripped of his garments
Leader: We adore you, O Christ, and we praise you.
All: Because by your cross you have redeemed the world.

> And Jesus said, "Father, forgive them, for they know not what they do." And they cast lots to divide his garments. (Luke 23:34 ESV)

Lord, you have borne so much, yet they add another level of humiliation. They strip you and leave you naked before the jeering crowds. Yet you respond in a way that does not make sense to your tormentors. You ask God to forgive them. You continue to love, even in the face of their abuse.

I so easily cut off people who offend me, Jesus. Without even being aware, I join a world that finds people to be disposable.

Forgive me for my unwillingness to let go of wrong done to me. Help me see people through your eyes of love.

Leader: Jesus Christ, Son of God
All: Have mercy on us.
All: Glory be to the Father, and to the Son, and to the Holy Spirit, as it was in the beginning, is now, and ever shall be, world without end. Amen.

Station 11—Jesus is nailed to the cross
Leader: We adore you, O Christ, and we praise you.
All: Because by your cross you have redeemed the world.

> And it was the third hour when they crucified him. And the inscription of the charge against him read, "The King of the Jews." And with him they crucified two robbers, one on his right and one on his left. And those who passed by derided him, wagging their heads and saying, "Aha! You who would destroy the temple and rebuild it in three days, save yourself, and come down from the cross!" So also, the chief priests with the scribes mocked him to one another, saying, "He saved others; he cannot save himself. Let the Christ, the King of Israel, come down now from the cross that we may see and believe." Those who were crucified with him also reviled him. (Mark 15:25–32 ESV)

Jesus, give us the strength to fathom what these final moments were like for you—to stretch out your hands and feet and have them nailed to the cross. And if the physical pain was not enough, the mocking of the crowds must have been unbearable. You bore this for me, Lord. Your love for me is without measure.

This level of love is beyond my reach. I am consumed by pettiness and judgment and selfishness. No, I cannot do it. A small measure of this love is only possible when I give myself fully to you as an instrument of your love. It is only then that I become a conduit of your love flowing through me.

Leader: Jesus Christ, Son of God
All: Have mercy on us.
All: Glory be to the Father, and to the Son, and to the Holy Spirit, as it was in the beginning, is now, and ever shall be, world without end. Amen.

Station 12—Jesus dies on the cross

Leader: We adore you, O Christ, and we praise you.
All: Because by your cross you have redeemed the world.

> Now from the sixth hour there was darkness over all the land until the ninth hour. And about the ninth hour Jesus cried out with a loud voice, saying, "Eli, Eli, lema sabachthani?" that is, "My God, my God, why have you forsaken me?" And some of the bystanders, hearing it, said, "This man is calling Elijah." And one of them at once ran and took a sponge, filled it with sour wine, and put it on a reed and gave it to him to drink. But the others said, "Wait, let us see whether Elijah will come to save him." And Jesus cried out again with a loud voice and yielded up his spirit.
>
> And behold, the curtain of the temple was torn in two, from top to bottom. And the earth shook, and the rocks were split. The tombs also were opened. And many bodies of the saints who had fallen asleep were raised, and coming out of the tombs after his resurrection they went into the holy city and appeared to many. When the centurion and those who were with him, keeping watch over Jesus, saw the earthquake and what

took place, they were filled with awe and said, "Truly this was the Son of God!" (Matt. 27:45–54 ESV)

Lord, thank you for this gift. Help me live a life worthy of your sacrifice.

Leader: Jesus Christ, Son of God
All: Have mercy on us.
All: Glory be to the Father, and to the Son, and to the Holy Spirit, as it was in the beginning, is now, and ever shall be, world without end. Amen.

Station 13—Jesus is taken down from the cross
Leader: We adore you, O Christ, and we praise you.
All: Because by your cross you have redeemed the world.

And when evening had come, since it was the day of Preparation, that is, the day before the Sabbath, Joseph of Arimathea, a respected member of the council, who was also himself looking for the kingdom of God, took courage and went to Pilate and asked for the body of Jesus. Pilate was surprised to hear that he should have already died. And summoning the centurion, he asked him whether he was already dead. And when he learned from the centurion that he was dead, he granted the corpse to Joseph. And Joseph bought a linen shroud, and taking him down, wrapped him in the linen shroud. (Mark 15:42–46a ESV)

Jesus, this would seem to be the end of your story. You have died and your body is now being cared for by a friend. It is his final act of devotion—to wash and clean your body and wrap it in a linen shroud—care designated for the wealthy. The crowd disperses, and the religious leaders congratulate each other on a victory won. Your followers are in deep despair as they grieve the loss of their leader and friend. No hope remains.

There are times, Lord, when I lose hope. I don't understand your ways and cannot comprehend that your plan may be different from my own. In these moments, remind me of this time when hope was gone and all seemed lost. But your ways are not those of the world, and unbeknownst to them, your greatest victory had been set in motion.

Leader: Jesus Christ, Son of God
All: Have mercy on us.
All: Glory be to the Father, and to the Son, and to the Holy Spirit, as it was in the beginning, is now, and ever shall be, world without end. Amen.

Station 14—Jesus is laid in the tomb

Leader: We adore you, O Christ, and we praise you.
All: Because by your cross you have redeemed the world.

> After these things Joseph of Arimathea, who was a disciple of Jesus, but secretly for fear of the Jews, asked Pilate that he might take away the body of Jesus, and Pilate gave him permission. So he came and took away his body. Nicodemus also, who earlier had come to Jesus by night, came bringing a mixture of myrrh and aloes, about seventy-five pounds in weight. So they took the body of Jesus and bound it in linen cloths with the spices, as is the burial custom of the Jews. Now in the place where he was crucified there was a garden, and in the garden a new tomb in which no one had yet been laid. So because of the Jewish day of Preparation, since the tomb was close at hand, they laid Jesus there. (John 19:38–42 ESV)

Lord, we have come to the end of the Way of Suffering. Your body is at rest, and the next chapter is about to begin. All creation holds its breath in anticipation of your victory. We come away from this time of devotion with a deeper understanding of your love. Give us the grace to be imitators of you. Fulfill our desire to enter into your work as instruments of love in this hurting world.

Leader: Jesus Christ, Son of God
All: Have mercy on us.
All: Glory be to the Father, and to the Son, and to the Holy Spirit, as it was in the beginning, is now, and ever shall be, world without end. Amen.

Concluding Thoughts

There has been criticism of the Stations of the Cross for ending at the tomb. Some would add a fifteenth station that depicts the resurrection of Christ. Yet that is not the purpose of the *Via Dolorosa*. The devotion offers a way to enter deeply into the suffering of Christ. It is tempting to move too quickly to the victory and bypass the struggle. The Stations of the Cross imitate life in recognizing the pain of living—which involves immense pain for many. The practice allows us to enter into the suffering of Christ and know that he is with us in every moment. He knows our pain.

Additional Resources

Jansen, Gary. *Station to Station: An Ignatian Journey through the Stations of the Cross*. Chicago: Loyola Press, 2016.
Pezzulo, Mary. *Meditations on the Way of the Cross*. Berkeley: Apocryphile Press, 2020.

Notes

[1] Herbert Thurston, *The Stations of the Cross: An Account of Their History and Devotional Purpose* (London: Burns & Oates, 1914), 4.

[2] Thurston, *The Stations of the Cross*, 6.

CHAPTER SEVENTEEN

Practicing the Presence

Contemplative prayer has as its goal a continual awareness of God's presence. It is opening oneself to whatever shaping God may want to do. It is a vulnerable stance to take before the living God. Each of the prayers in this guidebook seeks to assist the pray-er in listening. We let go of the agenda and prepare ourselves to receive. God knows us better than we know ourselves. When we submit, God will give us what is most needed.

We close with a prayer form that, in essence, is a culmination of all forms of contemplative prayer. It is living life with the intention of *practicing the presence of God*. Adele Calhoun defines it as "developing a rhythm of living that brings God to mind throughout the day."[1] Many throughout the centuries have dedicated their lives to this way of being. One simple lay brother from seventeenth-century France put words to the practice through correspondence with those who sought him out as a spiritual teacher.

Background and History

Carmelite monk Nicholas Herman, known as Brother Lawrence of the Resurrection, cultivated and practiced a life of continual awareness of the presence of God. As a young man from a simple family, he became a soldier in order to have food and shelter. The atrocities of what he saw and his actions deeply affected him. He saw no glory in what he had experienced. So, he chose to leave the life of a soldier in order to follow in the footsteps of an uncle who was a monk.

Brother Lawrence was a large man and somewhat clumsy. He was given a number of jobs, but due to his awkwardness, he was eventually placed in the kitchen. He served there as a cook for many years and then later became a sandal maker. Despite these simple vocations, he had a profound sense that all of one's life could be consecrated to God when lived with the awareness of God's presence. He "advocated a style of spirituality that developed a continual sense of being in God's presence, and the practice of returning to God's presence through deliberate acts of prayer."[2]

Many were drawn to Brother Lawrence because of his gentle ways and deep wisdom. Both the poor and esteemed held him in respect, and many sought his counsel. His correspondence and insights were collected following his death and put in the form of a book entitled *The Practice of the Presence of God*.

I first learned of Brother Lawrence when I was an undergraduate student. I had little exposure to the Christian disciplines outside of Bible study and intercessory prayer. This idea of practicing the presence of God captured my imagination. How logical! When I am aware that the God of the universe is with me, I live my life differently. The key is to remember. When I first learned about this practice, it got shuffled in with the other items on my "go-to-heaven" to-do list. I needed to force myself to practice the presence of God. Although this was good intent, I was missing part of the teaching of Brother Lawrence—we relinquish control through the disciplines. Practicing the Presence of God is not done by sheer willpower. It is a gift from God.

This way of being was marked by the listening side of prayer. God did the shaping as I made myself available for this grace. I didn't know it at the time, but Brother Lawrence was my introduction into the contemplative Christian disciplines.

PRACTICE

Brother Lawrence wrote, "This presence of God, though a bit painful in the beginning, if practiced faithfully works secretly in the soul and produces marvelous effects . . . and leads it insensibly to the simple grace, that loving sight of God everywhere present, which is the most holy, the most solid, the easiest, the most efficacious manner of prayer."[3]

Rather than being organized into steps that can then be followed, this prayer is a way of being. Other prayer forms assist in its accomplishment. We use the words of Brother Lawrence in his instruction on this continual state of divine awareness:

- The first way is purity of life.
- Second is faithfulness to an interior gaze on God—in other words, seeing God with one's imagination. This is to be done in a loving, quiet manner.
- Align your exterior actions with your interior gaze. Do this at the beginning, during your time of prayer, and at the end. Don't be discouraged when you get distracted. Maintain your intent to develop the habit. "Once you have acquired it, you will experience great joy."
- To maintain your focus on God, use phrases such as "My God, I am all yours," "God of love, I love you with all my heart," and "Lord, make me according to your heart."

- Let go of your attachment to worldly pleasures in order to be fully joined to the divine presence.

In essence, Brother Lawrence advocated (1) an intent to be pure of heart, (2) a practice of keeping God at the center of one's thoughts, (3) a commitment to living in such a way that is consistent with a pure heart, (4) a designation of words to chant to help maintain a focus on God, and (5) a release of one's attachment to the things of this world. He encouraged those he taught to follow these instructions daily. God would bring about a way of being that coincided with an awareness of his presence.

Additional Resources

Brother Lawrence of the Resurrection. *The Practice of the Presence of God: Writing and Conversations*, critical edition. Translated by Salvatore Sciurba. Washington, DC: ICS Publications, 2015.

Delaney, John, trans. *The Practice of the Presence of God by Brother Lawrence of the Resurrection*. New York: Doubleday & Co., 1977.

Elmer, Robert, and Brother Lawrence of the Resurrection. *Practicing God's Presence: Brother Lawrence for Today's Reader, Quiet Times for the Heart*. Colorado Springs, CO: NavPress, 2004.

Notes

[1] Adele Ahlberg Calhoun, *Spiritual Disciplines Handbook: Practices That Transform Us* (Downers Grove, IL: InterVarsity Press, 2015), 71.

[2] John R. Tyson, ed., *Invitation to Christian Spirituality: An Ecumenical Anthology* (Oxford: Oxford University Press, 1999), 19.

[3] John Delaney, trans., *The Practice of the Presence of God by Brother Lawrence of the Resurrection* (New York: Doubleday & Co., 1977), 110.

Rule of Life

It is a grace to have so many ways available to us to be with God. Each of the prayer forms in this guidebook can assist us in opening ourselves to God's shaping. It is important to try a number of forms to determine those that best resonate with you and help you lean into God's embrace. It is then critical to make them part of your rhythm of life—to establish a *rule of life* that allows you to center every aspect of your being on God.

Background and History

The *rule of life* is a term used for the codes created for monastic living. They are perhaps founded on the very first rule found in the second chapter of Acts: "They were continually devoting themselves to the apostles' teaching and to fellowship, to the breaking of bread and to prayer" (Acts 2:42 NASB). The rules written in the early days of the church looked to this structure. The most famous and widely used rule was written by Benedict of Nursia.

St. Benedict based his rule on Christ's instruction, "Therefore everyone who hears these words of Mine and acts on them, may be compared to a wise man who built his house on the rock" (Matt. 7:24 NASB). He sought to be intentional with grounding all aspects of monastic living on the teachings of Christ—first hearing them and then acting on them.[1] This involved a rhythm that included liturgical prayer, manual labor, and *Lectio Divina.* At the heart of the rule was a chapter on humility. Benedict said, "[O]bedience marked out the way to humility, and humility pointed the way to love; love was esteemed as the path to perfection."[2]

The intent of the monastic rule was to codify the monastic way of life and the hierarchy to which the monk committed obedience. The rule was a vehicle of continuity—not a legal document but an ethos. The prologue of the *Rule of Benedict* portrays this spirit in its opening lines: "Listen, oh my son, to the teachings of your master, and turn to them with the ear of your heart. Willingly accept the advice of a devoted father and put it into action."[3]

Although written to provide structure for life in a community, the *Rule of Benedict* offers a template for simplicity, humanity, and order in any life lived in devotion to God. This same intent is possible in contemporary existence, for all who seek to live with God at the center of their lives.

My introduction to a rule of life was when I was on a silent retreat. My heart's desire was to be a useful instrument of the kingdom—fully available for God's use. There were art supplies available, and I felt prompted to draw the various arenas of my life and color those that were dedicated for God's use. As I put it all down on paper, I realized that I tended to compartmentalize my spiritual life into a category separate from other areas of my life.

It spilled into some of the other aspects, such as my home life, but there were some that were obviously separate.

The speaker at the retreat was talking about Benedict's rule and a modern version entitled *Always We Begin Again*.[4] I instantly became enamored with the structured way of living articulated in the little book. It allowed all of one's life to be centered on Christ. I went back to my drawing and used the rule as a template with which to center every arena of my life on Christ. I wrote things down, dedicating myself to daily, weekly, monthly, and annual practices. Although I knew I would fall short of this promise, I made the commitment to dedicate my life in its pursuit.

PRACTICE

There are many ways to structure a rule of life. The merit lies in the creation and commitment to its practices.

Creating It Alone

The following is a method with a holistic focus:

- Draw a chart with four arenas: physical, intellectual, relational, and spiritual.
- Under each of these arenas, write daily, weekly, monthly, and annual practices.
  - These are similar to New Year's resolutions but with the intent of dedicating the practice to God.
- Spend time in prayer, asking God to be with you in the process.
- As you fill out your rule, only include items that are non-negotiable. They may be practices that are already part of your life that you want to offer to God.
- When finished with the rule, eliminate half of what you have written.

- ■ This will be difficult but is important to the exercise.
- ■ You can do things not on the chart, but you want to ensure you've included the practices that are most important to you.
- After a few months, reevaluate to ensure that your rule contains those practices to which you are truly committed.
- On an annual basis, pray over and recommit to your practices.

Leading a Group

When leading a group, project a chart on a screen or draw one on a whiteboard. Fill in the categories along the top and the time periods down the side (an example is provided on the next pages). You can either provide a chart for each participant to fill in or have them copy the example on the screen or whiteboard. Give the following instructions:

- "Under each of these arenas, write daily, weekly, monthly, and annual practices. These are similar to New Year's resolutions but with the intent of dedicating the practice to God."
- "Before you begin filling in your chart, spend a few moments asking God to be with you in the process."
- "As you choose what to place in your chart, only include items that are nonnegotiable. They may be practices that are already part of your life that you want to offer to God or may be practices that you want to begin."

Give participants about ten minutes to work on the rule. Continue with the following:

- "Now eliminate half of what you have included."

- "This is difficult but is important to ensure you are just including practices to which you are willing to commit."
- "You can do things not on the chart, but you want to ensure you've included the practices that are most important to you."
- "This is just the beginning. Wait a few days and reevaluate your rule. Make adjustments—again, retaining only those practices that are nonnegotiable."
- "We're now going to share some of our rules. Share only what you want to share."

Have participants first share with a small group of four to five. Then call the entire gathering together for a time of sharing with the entire group. The following is an example of a rule of life:

	Physical	Relational	Intellectual	Spiritual
Daily	• Eight glasses of water a day • Five servings of fruits and vegetables • Protein	• Compliment my spouse	• Check on world events	• Anglican prayer beads • Centering prayer • Scripture
Weekly	• Cardio five times a week • Strength building three times	• Check in with my daughters • Dedicate one day of the week in prayer for each family member • Date with spouse • Coffee or lunch with one friend	• Read a book for pleasure • Write a blog post	• Worship with my faith community • Centering prayer group • Bible study

	Physical	Relational	Intellectual	Spiritual
Monthly	• Outside activity such as hiking or kayaking	• Extended date with spouse • In-depth conversation with each child	• Write a larger project • Participate in learning something new • Read a book for professional development	• Spiritual directors peer group • Extended time (half-day or day) with God
Annual	• Annual checkup	• Family vacation • Marriage summit	• Create a new course for non-profit	• Eight-day silent retreat

As mentioned previously, be strict on committing to only those practices that are nonnegotiable. You can make changes after you live with the rule for a time, but you don't want to give up because you have made it impossible to follow. Live with it for a while—a month or so—and then revisit it. After you have settled on your rule of life, revisit it on an annual basis. Like the Sabbath, the rule was made for people; people weren't made for the rule.

Concluding Thoughts

The practice of disciplines is not accidental. They happen only with intention and then action. As with the analogy of the stream, it is only when we are still that the silt settles and we are able to see clearly. We must first make ourselves available and then God can shape us into useful instruments of the kingdom.

Additional Resources

Barton, Ruth Haley. *Sacred Rhythms: Arranging Our Lives for Spiritual Transformation.* Downers Grove, IL: InterVarsity Press, 2006.

de Waal, Esther. *Seeking God: The Way of St. Benedict.* Collegeville, MN: Liturgical Press, 1984.

McQuiston, John, II, and Phyllis Tickle. *Always We Begin Again: The Benedictine Way of Living,* revised edition. New York: Morehouse, 2011.

Notes

[1] John R. Tyson, ed., *Invitation to Christian Spirituality: An Ecumenical Anthology* (Oxford: Oxford University Press, 1999), 24.

[2] Tyson, *Invitation to Christian Spirituality,* 125.

[3] Esther de Waal, *Seeking God: The Way of St. Benedict* (Collegeville, MN: Liturgical Press, 1984), 28.

[4] John McQuiston II and Phyllis Tickle, *Always We Begin Again: The Benedictine Way of Life,* rev. ed. (New York: Morehouse, 2011).

Acknowledgments

What a joy to have opportunity to acknowledge those who have played key roles in my journey with contemplative prayer. It began as a child with parents who taught me to love God and relish his presence. It was fostered in a church that has at its heart a love for Christ and the Word and a desire to share that love with the world.

Teachers, both informal and formal, have taught me through the script of their lives—showing me Christ when the doubts of a developing faith would draw me away. I am grateful to Jesuit friends who help me know God as love and for extended family members who are dedicated to living as instruments of God.

But most of all, I am grateful for my family. My daughters, Erin and Ashley, who continue to amaze me with their graciousness, sense of humor, and considerable gifts, and to my life partner, Randy, whose life speaks of God's goodness. He is a man who not only speaks of loving this hurting world, but consistently walks alongside the marginalized. I have had the distinct privilege of living with this man for the past thirty-nine years. He has supported me, counseled me, and loved me without condition. He has picked up the slack, without complaint, time and again as I took on yet another project. This book could not have come to fruition without him.

Finally, I cannot neglect to thank my God. It is my deepest hope that this book will help others come away with a glimpse of God's fathomless love. It is a love that is beyond understanding. I cannot express my gratitude for the small morsel I have tasted.